All in a Lifetime

All in a Lifetime

By
Edgar A. Guest

Granger Index Reprint Series

BOOKS FOR LIBRARIES PRESS
FREEPORT, NEW YORK

First Published 1938
Reprinted 1970

PS3513
U45
A78
1970

~~811~~
~~G936aL~~

INTERNATIONAL STANDARD BOOK NUMBER:
0-8369-6201-X

LIBRARY OF CONGRESS CATALOG CARD NUMBER:
76-133071

PRINTED IN THE UNITED STATES OF AMERICA

DEDICATED

TO ALL THE FRIENDS
OF A LIFETIME

—Edgar A. Guest

INDEX

Index

Index

Index

Index

Index

ALL IN A LIFETIME

Life holds so much variety
  Before death shuts his eyes,
A man can work and hope to be
  Clever and rich and wise;

Loyal and honest, brave and true,
  Cheerful and broad of mind;
Strong for the tasks he has to do;
  Patient, considerate, kind.

And life will hold and always will
  Unto the journey's end
Such posts as these for him to fill:
  Brother, neighbor, friend;

Husband and father, and to some
  An uncle's role he'll play
And later on he may become
  A grandsire, old and gray.

The lives of many each must touch,
  So varied is life's plan,
We seldom realize how much
  It takes to be a man.

THEY'RE LAUGHING NOW

They're laughing now! And strangest thing,
About the old dead worrying
And fretful times they used to know,
Back in that vanished long ago
When they were married first, and he
Had just his weekly salary.

You'd think 'twas fun, to hear them say
How he would walk to work each day
To save the car fare and afraid
They couldn't get their gas bill paid.
And how they worked for months before
They had a rug upon the floor.

And they are boasting, too, about
The time he wore his trousers out
And she put in a patch so small
You'd hardly notice it at all.
He loves to tell that tale again,
Although it wasn't funny then!

They're laughing now! And seems to me
The old dead cares have grown to be
Their happiest memories of all,
As if there's nothing to recall
So sweet as all those troubles grave
When love was young and very brave.

THE TRICK

I noticed as soon as I opened the door
   That the fellow was surly, and so
With a frown just as black as the one that he wore
   I angrily told him to go.
Now, I hadn't the slightest intention to be
As surly, uncivil and hateful as he,
But that was the trick that he played upon me.

Another chap came to my doorstep that day,
   And a twinkle he had in his eye.
With a smile on his face, he began in a way
   That prompted a gentle reply.
Though a stranger he was, I was eager to be
As gracious, good-natured and kindly as he,
And that was the trick that he played upon me.

Since those visits, I've thought in this life that we
     live,
   And the lesson seems simple to learn,
We get back a smile for the smile that we give,
   And a frown brings a frown in return.
If I chuckle, with chuckles I'll surely be met.
Just as I set my lips, so all lips will be set,
And that is a trick that I musn't forget.

TO ALL PARENTS

"I'll lend you for a little time a child of Mine," He
    said,
"For you to love the while she lives and mourn for
    when she's dead.
It may be six or seven years, or twenty-two or three,
But will you, till I call her back, take care of her
    for Me?
She'll bring her charms to gladden you, and shall
    her stay be brief
You'll have her lovely memories as solace for your
    grief.

"I cannot promise she will stay, since all from earth
    return,
But there are lessons taught down there I want this
    child to learn.
I've looked the wide world over in my search for
    teachers true
And from the throngs that crowd life's lanes I have
    selected you.
Now will you give her all your love, nor think the
    labor vain,
Nor hate Me when I come to call to take her back
    again?"

I fancied that I heard them say: "Dear Lord, Thy
    will be done!
For all the joy Thy child shall bring, the risk of
    grief we'll run.

We'll shelter her with tenderness, we'll love her
while we may,
And for the happiness we've known forever grate-
ful stay;
But shall the angels call for her much sooner than
we've planned,
We'll brave the bitter grief that comes and try to
understand."

❧   ❧   ❧

THE FEMININE TOUCH

If it were not for woman's care
Houses would ugly be and bare.
Few men would ever think to sweep
Or curtains at the windows keep.

A MEAL-TIME REACTIONARY

Since the slices grow thinner and thinner,
  And the rules of the table demand
Seven courses of froth for a dinner
  Served up in the manner called grand,
Sometimes in rebellion I mutter:
  "Can't we give up the fads for awhile
And dish up the bread and the butter
  In the old-fashioned family style?

"Get a red cloth with fringe for the table,
  Stand the celery stalks in a glass.
Find a cruet, if still you are able,
  With peppers and salts we can pass.
Pile up the bread on a platter,
  Have teaspoons end-up in a jar.
Why is dining so solemn a matter
  That afraid to be natural we are?

"Bring out the pickles and spices.
  Let all our hot victuals behold.
What if the new method nice is,
  Why should the murphies grow cold?
Let shimmery jellies and wavy
  Entice us and tempt as we wait.
What's wrong with passing the gravy
  As soon as we've meat on the plate?

"Where have the napkin rings vanished?
  Why have the toothpicks been banned?

Why was the butter dish banished?
  Why can't the food be on hand?"
Oh, I may be a back-sliding sinner
  That follows no rule book or guide,
But I long for that old-fashioned dinner
  Our grandmothers used to provide.

❧   ❧   ❧

THE ABSENTEE

The man was old; the maiden young
And gifted with a flattering tongue.
Dan Cupid on their wedding day
Deliberately stayed away.

BURNING CANDLE

I watched a candle burning at a banquet table spread,
Adding just a touch of beauty by the mellow light it
shed,
But strangely in the center was the tallest of the lot,
Which was purposely unlighted or by chance had
been forgot.

The burning candles glistened; every lovely beam
they threw
Brought them nearer to their death beds when
they'd die as candles do,
But the one they'd left unlighted stayed a golden
taper tall,
Still retaining all its freshness, giving out no light
at all.

Then I wondered as I watched them, are we all
like candles made,
With the gift of light within us, but to use it up
afraid?
Do we hope that life may miss us and, forgetful,
pass us by
While our fellows burn in service for the joy they
can supply?

FISHERMAN'S SOLITUDE

Where is it man can slip alone
    And shut the world away,
An hour of solitude to own,
    To think and dream and pray?

At home in moments most profound,
    Locked door and drawn the shade,
The jangling telephone will sound
    To call him back to trade.

One haunt is left for solemn moods,
    High thoughts and lofty dreams.
Men still respect the solitudes
    Of woods and running streams.

The fisherman who leaves the land
    May call that hour his own,
For all his kind will understand
    His wish to be alone.

They'll wave, perhaps, in passing by,
    But, like a man at prayer
Communing with his God on high
    They'll leave him dreaming there.

WIVES

A wife is one who lifts from chairs
The hat and coat her husband wears;
Who cleans the bathroom day by day
And puts his razor blades away.
She finds pajamas on the floor
And hangs them on the closet door.
She takes her shirts and studs and ties
And hides them right beneath his eyes,
That, when he's hunted near and far,
He'll find them where they always are.

A wife is one who understands
The endless care a man demands.
Though fully grown, she comes to see
That still in much a child is he.
He must be babied, petted, pleased,
And never criticized or teased.
He must be flattered and admired;
Be pitied when he's ill or tired
And when he has an aching head
With tenderness be put to bed.

A wife is one by duty bound
To think her husband most profound.
If she with him would get along
She must pretend he's never wrong.
However foolish he may be
With all he says she must agree

For, once she points his follies out,
For days the dear old thing will pout.
To every wife this praise is due:
Hers is a job no man could do.

❧ ❧ ❧

HUSBANDS

A husband is the fellow that a wife must drag about
And battle with at evening when it's time to take
him out.
He's the chap you see at operas with that vacant,
patient stare
That announces very plainly that his wife has hauled
him there.
You can see the music bores him and you know the
dear old grouch
Would much rather she had left him to lie snoring
on the couch.

A husband is the fellow that a wife must scheme
and plan
To exhibit on occasions just to prove she has a man.
She must take him out to socials, lectures, literary
teas
And display him to the people, though he's plainly
ill at ease.

He's the meek and patient mortal with the shiny
    hairless dome
Who sits idly in some corner till it's time to take
    him home.

A husband is the duty-loving martyr for a cause
Who thinks he suffers tortures without glory or
    applause.
He's the man the concert doorman knows the minute
    that he sees
By that tell-tale look upon him of "it's anything to
    please!"
He's the fellow in the ballroom with that solemn
    gaze and glum
Who hides out with twenty others who would
    rather not have come.

❧ ❧ ❧

MY CHOICE

Some wish, while history they con,
They'd known the heroes dead and gone,
But I would rather know instead
Bill Jones alive than Caesar dead.

ROADSIDE TABLE

I wonder have you noticed them along the highway
    shining—
Those "Roadway Table" signs which mark the beau-
    ty spots for dining?
Of all the boards which edge the road there's none
    more fascinating
Than those which tell the passing throng the dinner
    table's waiting.

They twinkle in the morning sun; with joy they
    fairly glisten;
They tell of singing birds nearby and bid man to
    stop to listen.
They hint of elm and maple trees and breezes soft
    and tender
And ask who will to take his meal in groves of peace
    and splendor.

I read the signs along the way designed to warn
    the stranger
And some proclaim that curves are near and some
    are shrieking "danger!"
Well pleased am I to heed them all, as far as I am
    able,
But most alluring is the one that signals: "Roadside
    Table."

I never pass that gentle shield but gratefully I read
    it,

I know that beauty waits nearby for all who care
    to heed it.
I'm sure no happier message comes by letter, air or
    cable
Than that which flashes from the sign announcing:
    "Roadside Table."

      ⚜ ⚜ ⚜

THE REAL SPORT

The fun is in the winning, not the spending,
    The doing, not in trinkets of reward,
Though all in vict'ry wish the battle ending,
    The thrill is in the swinging of the sword.

The joy is in the race and not the cheering,
    The struggle, not the comment in the press;
The keeping on in spite of all the fearing.
    The thrill is in the battle for success.

The sport is in the doing and the daring,
    The prize is just a lure to catch the eye,
To live is to be fighting odds and caring,
    To rest and feel no sadness is to die.

THE RAILROAD ENGINEER

Because at fifty miles he drives
And may endanger human lives,
They test his hearing and his sight,
His heart and lungs and appetite.
They even search his family tree
For traces of insanity.
If liquor on his breath they smell
They call him in and say: "Farewell!
No longer fit to drive are you!
Too great the risk! Pack up! You're through!"

Before they grant to him the power
To drive at fifty miles an hour,
His every faculty they test
To know that he is at his best.
The regulations he must learn
Regarding every stop and turn.
They teach him that the right of way
Has signals which he must obey.
If once he breaks the safety code
They promptly take him off the road.

Does he face danger every day?
And where he drives do children play?
Are sick men, lame men apt to tread
The path he travels just ahead?
Must he expect such risks to meet
As motorists on every street

That those who hire him still demand
A sober brain and steady hand?
Oh, no! His path is fairly clear;
But he's a railroad engineer!

❧ ❧ ❧

AGE TALKS TO YOUTH

Old age whispered: "Youth, beware!
Love will lead you into care.

"When the glamor disappears
Lovers wake to sighs and tears.

"Love is duty, love is pain,
Sacrifice and loss and gain.

"Look at us, grown old and gray;
Would you fade the self-same way?

"Would you have your features wear
Such deep-graven lines of care?"

"Yes," said youth, "for that we pray.
We would fade the self-same way.

"All that you have known of care,
Pain and anguish we would share.

"And when grown as old as you
May we be as wrinkled, too."

THE SIDEWALKS OF LIFE

Up and down the sidewalks romp the children at
their play
While in and out among them walk the weary folks
and gray,
And in and out among them walk the seekers after
fame,
But I think the while I watch them, they are very
much the same.

The little girls are wheeling waxen dollies up and
down,
The little boys are soldiers on their way to sack a
town,
But the older women trundle real babies in the sun
And are doing for a purpose what the children do
for fun.

The little men and women have their cares and sor-
rows, too,
They suffer disappointments, as the weary grown-ups
do.
There are bickerings and quarrels on the sidewalks
every day
Which sound very like the wranglings of the wrin-
kled brows and gray.

Up and down the sidewalks romp the children at
their play

While in and out among them grown-ups hurry on
    their way;
And I think the while I watch them, when life's
    story's fully told,
The burdens of the children are the burdens of the
    old.

❦   ❦   ❦

ARGUMENT

The dandelion to the daisy said:
    "There is no Heaven for you,
Who would be crowned when he is dead
    Must wear a golden hue."

The timid daisy answered low:
    "In spotless white we're dressed
That all upon the earth may know
    God loves the daisies best!"

A cynic bee who passed that way
    Said: "What poor fools are these!
It makes no difference how they pray,
    Heaven is reserved for bees."

"We shall in glory stand arrayed
    When this brief life is gone,
Flowers are but things our God has made
    For us to feed upon!"

THE DIFFERENCE

He was a king for an hour or two,
  Playing from town to town;
Lived, as he fancied a king must do;
  Wearing his robes and crown.

Subjects knelt at his golden throne.
  Flatterers hailed his name.
There was a castle he called his own
  Till the fall of the curtain came.

"Every inch a king!" the critics said.
  "Nobly he plays the part.
The royal lines are truly read
  With feeling and perfect art."

Now the king had heard of this actor's skill
  And he thought he would like to see
How an artist handled the royal will
  And just what a king should be.

He sat through the play till the curtain fell
  But said as he turned away,
  "I believe as a king I could do as well
  For only two hours a day!

"When he goes home he can romp and play
  And put all his glory by,
He can live his life in his chosen way
  But always a king am I."

33

THE GAIN

When life was bright and cheerful he went singing
    on his way.
He scarcely knew his neighbors or what sort of folks
    were they.
But he woke one dismal morning to find all his
    money gone,
And he found that fame and fortune were not safe
    to lean upon.

The other day I met him, and he said: "It's very
    queer,
But the fact is I am happier than I've been for many
    a year.
I've discovered friendly people living just across the
    street;
I've discovered books and blossoms and the grass be-
    neath my feet.

"Since the bank account has dwindled I've discovered
    at my door
A variety of blessings which I'd never known before.
I've discovered chess and checkers are not games
    which children play,
But are glorious entertainment when at home you
    choose to stay.

"Oh, we're richer now in spirit than we ever thought
    we'd be,

There's a bond of true devotion binding all the
    family.
We have gained in faith and wisdom and in fellow-
    ship with flowers.
And whatever loss may follow, these shall evermore
    be ours."

❧ ❧ ❧

WHAT I WANT

I don't want a pipe and I don't want a watch.
I don't want cigars or a bottle of Scotch.
I don't want a thing that your money can buy.
I don't want a shirt or a four-in-hand tie.
If you really would make this old heart of mine glad,
I just want to know you're still fond of your dad.

You women folks say, and believe it I can,
"It's so terribly hard to buy things for a man!"
And from all that I've heard I am sure it must be.
Well, I don't want you spending your money on me.
The joy that I crave in a store can't be had.
I just want to know you're still fond of your dad.

Get on with your shopping; give others the stuff!
For me just a hug and a kiss are enough!
Just come in at Christmas with love in your eye
And tell me you think I'm a pretty swell guy.
With that for my gift I can never be sad.
I just want to know you're still fond of your dad.

THE THINGS ETERNAL

If life be nothing but a fight
For food; a place to sleep at night,
  And fire and robes to wear;
If growth be nothing more than size,
And age be merely dimming eyes,
  Then death's the end of care.

If men, like bugs and flies and worms,
But live their days on nature's terms
  And in her process die,
Then brute and beast, who eat and drink,
Are better off than men who think
  And often sit and sigh.

But age with joy a book can thumb
And dream of ampler years to come,
  And under every care
And back of hurt of every kind,
The thoughtful man can solace find
  Which softens his despair.

Long after nature's growth is done
A growth in wisdom still goes on,
  With its attendant peace,
And something hints that worldly strife
Is but the gateway to a life
  Where growth shall never cease.

CITY PIGEONS

I watched them from the windows, common pigeons
    in a flock,
Who make their nests in nooks of stone which line
    a city block,
And I wondered, with the country fresh and green
    not far away,
Why there among the haunts of trade those birds
    prefer to stay.

No blade of grass is left them and no warm, fresh
    earth to tread!
Today the sun is shining and blue skies are over-
    head,
But the city pigeons linger in cathedral aisles of
    gloom
And seem to be contented where no tree comes into
    bloom.

It would seem that birds of freedom would not linger
    in the town,
Where all is cold and harsh and grim, and men rush
    up and down,
But winter comes to woodland and snow the valley
    fills,
And gentle folks in buildings tall strew crumbs on
    window sills:

For as I watched and pondered I saw across the way

37

A woman place some bits of bread upon the granite
gray,
And all the pigeons knew her and knew the meal
was good,
And why they choose to stay in town I think I
understood.

   ❧   ❧   ❧

THE MEANING OF LOSS

He tossed it on a rubbish heap,
  Contented to forsake it;
A thing he didn't want to keep,
  But not a soul would take it.

He put it under lock and key
  Endeavoring to conceal it.
'Twas very dear to him and he
  Feared thieves would try to steal it.

Our richest joys we cannot keep.
  We know they all must perish,
But things upon life's rubbish heap
  We neither love nor cherish.

So by the sorrows all must share
  The depths of love we measure.
The harder seems the loss to bear
  The richer was the treasure.

HOME INGREDIENTS

If it's only just a shelter from the rain and winter
    snow;
If it's only just a place to sleep when over-tired you
    grow;
If it's just a place to pack your bag when you de-
    cide to roam,
It may be a handsome building, but it's truly not
    a home.

If it's just a place to eat in when you're not invited
    out;
If you're snapping at the children every time they
    romp about;
If you never, proud and happy walk its garden in
    the gloam,
You may have a house to look at, but you haven't
    made a home.

If it's just a place to dwell in, not to rest and read
    and stay;
If the children very early choose to go elsewhere to
    play;
If the neighbors' understanding of their needs ex-
    ceeds your own,
Though you give them food and shelter, still a home
    they've never known.

QUESTIONING

Forever man questions life's meaning, and never
there comes a reply.
Forever he shatters the silence with "What am I
doing and why?"
He seeks for some loftier purpose which never he's
able to find;
Some ultimate goal which he fancies may give him
contentment of mind.

He discovers that pleasure is fleeting; the joy of
achievement is small;
That men in high places grow weary and sick of
the sham of it all;
That life is but eating and drinking and working
the long years away
And little is altered or bettered, let him struggle
however he may.

So simply this life has been fashioned that never
believe it we can
That all this old earth has to offer is the common
experience of man;
That bearing his burdens with courage, being patient
and kindly and true,
And sharing his joys with his fellows is all that God
wants him to do.

DRESSING UP

When she was only three or four
  She played at being grown,
And oft her mother's garments wore,
  As though they were her own.
She strutted in a trailing dress
  And wore a bonnet gay.
For that was Janet's happiness
  On many a rainy day.

She loved the game of dressing up
  And having friends for tea.
The way she held her little cup
  Was proper as could be.
For capes and robes and pretty things
  She robbed both hook and shelf.
Took brooches, bracelets, pins and rings
  And hung them on herself.

I've chuckled many a rainy day
  To see her thus attired
And have her curtsey low and say:
  "Your company is desired.
A few friends I have asked for tea.
  I've known them all my life;
And very happy I should be
  If you should bring your wife."

Now to those grand and lofty airs
  Has Janet fully grown,

And still her mother's trinkets wears,
    As though they were her own.
But what is more than silk and lace
    And jeweled neck and arms,
She also wears with youthful grace
    Her mother's many charms.

❧ ❧ ❧

THE TEST

God did not test him in the open space
    Where men could see,
But in the quiet of a secret place,
    Alone was he.

And watching there was neither friend nor foe
    Of whom to be afraid.
None other but himself on earth to know
    The choice he made.

If ever it were safe to sin, 'twas then,
    But tempted so,
He said: "Though I deceive my fellowmen,
    I still shall know!

"I still shall have to face myself each day
    Though none may know.
I will not have my shaving mirror say:
    'Hey, cheat! Hello!'"

UNDOING A COLLEGE EDUCATION

One time there was a college boy, an honor student,
    too,
Who thought he ought to show the folks at home
    how much he knew.
With scorn for this and scorn for that, he filled his
    father's ear,
For having gathered knowledge he had also learned
    to sneer.

The youngster went about the town with a most
    superior air,
He couldn't stand the manners of the old friends
    living there.
He hated this and hated that; with a frown upon
    his face,
He called the neighbors vulgar and their notions
    commonplace.

One evening as they sat alone his troubled father
    said:
"I sent you down to college to gain wisdom, but
    instead,
Unto my sorrow and dismay I find on your return,
You've merely picked up tricks of pride which any
    boor can learn.

"You needn't go to college to discover things to hate.
To sneer at human failings is an art not very great.

The faults of other people even ignorant men can
　　find—
Now take this tip from father—any fool can be
　　unkind."

※　※　※

FINAL JUDGMENT

Sometimes the cleverest err;
　　Sometimes the strongest fail.
God may the weak prefer
　　When ended is life's tale.

The eyes of men are blind
　　To much that God must see.
The fault that mortals find
　　To Him no fault may be.

The failure to succeed,
　　Which on the earth is plain,
May, by His purpose, lead
　　To everlasting gain.

On earth lives none so wise
　　Along life's baffling way
Of anyone who dies
　　To know what God will say.

THE LITTLE SICK GIRL

The little sick child doesn't get in the way
Or bring in the neighboring children to play.
The house is as still as a church on a Monday,
And thought 'tis a week day it seems just like Sunday.
    For everything's neat
    And her gay little feet
Aren't tracking the parlor with mud from the street.

The little sick child isn't racing about;
It seems like a year since we last heard her shout.
Without interruption to talk now we're able.
There's no one at meals to spill milk on the table.
    From morning till night
    Everything is just right,
And yet in perfection we find no delight.

It doesn't take long when a little one's ill
To weary of rooms that are tidy and still.
The day quickly comes when you'd give all your
    gold for
The racket and noise which so often you scold for.
    For that obstinate spell
    And that clamorous yell,
And that trouble she makes are the signs that she's
    well.

LOVE AFFAIR

I saw him on a topmost limb, a strutting of his stuff,
And watching from my window, thought "a lover
    sure enough!"
A lover singing serenades to woo his lady fair.
I wonder if she's somewhere near with eyes upon
    him there.

He sang as though his throat would burst. I thought
    I'd like to know
If she with favor smiled on him or had some other
    beau.
The air was filled with rapturous song. No sign I
    saw her make.
I wondered was there someone else that she pre-
    ferred to take.

He hopped about from twig to twig, quite plainly
    showing off,
A handsome scarlet cardinal at which no maid could
    scoff.
And when at last I left him there still singing on the
    limb,
I hoped that maid he wanted so would give her
    heart to him.

THE TRICKSTER

He had wit and he was clever,
  He was sharp and he was slick,
But no man can live forever
  On the magic of a trick.
It may work when first you do it,
But in time the crowd sees through it.

Soon the word was passed about him:
  "When that fellow near you stands
Never trust him, always doubt him,
  Watch his fingers, watch his hands!"
Thus by warnings wise preceded
Cleverer, smarter tricks he needed.

What seemed easy now grew irksome,
  But he scorned the ways of men,
Still believing he could work some
  Bit of cunning now and then.
But, though cleverly he plotted,
Everybody had him spotted.

Times are tough and growing tougher,
  Here he is at thirty-six
Just another clever duffer
  Absolutely out of tricks.
And the years which lie before him
Hold a sorry prospect for him.

UNPURCHASABLE

A rich man called his son aside
And said: "The money I'll provide.
To an unlimited amount
I'll guarantee your bank account.
Go out and walk the market's length
And buy yourself a stock of strength,
As men buy rifles, so that you
Can bear as much as others do.

"Then while you're shopping keep in mind
You'll need the very finest kind
Of courage, so make sure to buy
The best the market can supply.
If strength and pluck are shown for sale,
Buy every barrel, jug and pail
Which you may chance to see displayed,
And gladly will the bill be paid.

"Go out and pay whate'er you will
To any master for his skill
And bribe a scholar to dispose
Of every helpful fact he knows.
Flourish your gold where all may see
And cry: "I'll buy integrity!
My character is worn and frayed,
I seek a new one, ready made.'"

The youngster left and round about
The startled merchants heard him shout:

"Good gold for courage offered here!
For brains I'll pay a million clear!
Who'll sell me strength that I may hold
My own against the brave and bold?"
But those who heard him thought him daft
Or pitied him or merely laughed.

❧ ❧ ❧

VICTORY

What does it matter, after all,
That some have more and others less?
Men often give their best and fall
And die and never know success.
Heaven will be filled with creatures odd
If only victories count with God.

I've felt the scorn a failure knows,
But here's the thought reflection brings:
Must man be master of his foes?
Was he designed for winning things?
When to the cross His hands were nailed
Many imagined Christ had failed.

What if the dream be unfulfilled?
What if the goal be ne'er attained?
There must be something which we build
Outlasting treasure lost or gained.
What man calls triumph cannot be
God's final test of victory.

A RABBIT MOVES IN

There's a little jack rabbit comes into our garden
With never a "May I?" or "Begging your pardon!"
Or "Please, sir, permit me. I'm hungry for roots."
And he nibbles the green leaves and tender young
    shoots,
And I vow that I'll send for a shotgun and end him—
Which I would, didn't Janet rise up to befriend
    him.

I've seen him go leaping my rose garden over;
I've seen him devouring my choicest of clover;
I've caught him—the rascal—at work on my phlox,
And I know he has eaten my best hollyhocks!
Already he's cost me nine dollars in money—
But Janet insists he's a cute little bunny.

Now, I wouldn't mind it so much if this rabbit
Had asked my permission my grounds to inhabit;
But he didn't! He moved in one bright starry night
As if to my shrubs he'd a God-given right.
And I swear that I'd fix him so he couldn't fret me
By nibbling my posies—if Janet would let me.

OLD GRAY-BEARD ANNUALS

The middle-aged perennials with all their labor done
Are gossiping like women in the warm October sun.
I think I hear them saying: "Grandpa Zinnia's very
 low
And the frost will surely take him in another day
 or so."

I walk about the garden in the early morning haze
To see the gray-beard annuals whose years are told
 in days.
Their youth is of the springtime and their prime is
 of July,
But now it is October and they're old and soon to
 die.

The annuals late in autumn seem like people late in
 life,
All scarred and bruised by struggle and completely
 used by strife.
And, like the neighboring women when an old
 man's pulse runs low,
I think I hear the larkspur say: "It's sad to watch
 them go!"

THE OLD-TIME SITTING ROOM

We used to have a parlor, in the days when we
    were small,
Which was entered from a doorway at the right
    side of the hall,
And the parlor was for company, and the times we
    made a fuss;
But next there was the sitting room—and that room
    was for us.

The parlor seemed all mystery! Not oft we got in
    there.
The mother fashioned covers to go over every chair.
On very rare occasions was the door flung open
    wide,
And we sat very stiff and straight when once we
    got inside.

I have a recollection there were pictures on the wall
Of people dignified and old, I never knew at all.
The room seemed rather solemn just because it held
    so much
Of sacred family treasures that we weren't allowed
    to touch.

The sitting room was different—I still see the oval
    frames
Which held the crayon portraits of my uncles, George
    and James;

And my mother's little rocker where beside the stove
    she sat,
And the spot upon the sofa that belonged unto the
    cat.

It seemed always overcrowded, as I recollect it now,
But it held a lot of gladness for the old and young,
    somehow.
And perhaps today what's needed, in these times of
    doubt and gloom,
Is a little of the courage of that family sitting room.

❧   ❧   ❧

FAME

Fame pays no heed to birth or place.
    She keeps no favorite haunts in mind.
The gifted children of the race
    She'll journey far and wide to find.

The rich upon their own bestow
    What they have gained by toil and thrift,
But fame to cabin doors will go
    For talent is a rarer gift.

Wherever men of merit dwell
    And nobly used are thought and skill,
Fame will come ringing at the bell
    And set them on the topmost hill.

TWO WINDOWS

My office window looks on brick and steel and
    granite stone
And pavements hard and cold and gray where only
    trade is known.
I look between the buildings tall and all I see is
    strife
And wonder if such wearying care is all there is to
    life.

There's little beauty in the scene my office window
    frames.
One wearies reading printed signs and gold-leaf
    blazoned names.
And did I catch no broader view than this I daily
    see,
I'd wonder if this world is what God fashioned it
    to be.

But in my little room at home, safe settled in my
    chair,
I look another window through and loveliness is
    there.
The grass is green, the flowers are bright, the birds
    are on the wing,
And I discover life is not a cold and sordid thing.

All nature's charms are on display; the children
    romp about,

The people passing up and down seem happy to be
    out.
And looking at earth's gentler scenes, the thought
    occurs to me
How small the view of life my office window lets
    me see.

❧ ❧ ❧

AFTERWARDS

This was the prayer that oft we made
    And thought it made in vain:
That God, his faltering strength to aid,
    Would let us share his pain.

We who had strength for every task
    That strength with him would share.
Nightly we turned to Him to ask
    What he no more could bear.

Day after day we pleaded thus:
    Lord, can you not release
Some of his cruel pain to us
    That he may rest in peace?

God heard! A calm is on his brow,
    And as we made our prayer
He sweetly sleeps tonight, but now
    The pain is ours to bear.

BALLAD OF A CARELESS MAN

Of things that women do and must,
   I know 'tis useless to complain.
It is their joy to sweep and dust
   And rise at dawn to sweep again.
The least disorder gives them pain,
   But I have methods of my own
And, though I know the wish is vain,
   I wish they'd leave my desk alone!

In mop and broom they place their trust.
   From dawn till day begins to wane
They battle dirt and signs of rust,
   Grim foes of fingerprint and stain.
They straighten out the counterpane
   On which my linen soiled I've thrown,
But this small favor would I gain:
   I wish they'd leave my desk alone!

All things of mine away they thrust.
   There's nothing I can long retain.
To my despair and my disgust,
   Their "tidying up" I can't restrain.
A thousand times I've made it plain,
   Though high the litter stack has grown,
Untouched I want it to remain.
   I wish they'd leave my desk alone!

L'Envoi—

I know how women work and strain

That order everywhere shall reign,
But still I make this anguished groan:
I wish they'd leave my desk alone!

THE SALESMAN

He came to the door with a wink in his eye
  And a trace of a grin on his lips.
A peddler of something he wished I would buy
  Which he carried about in his grips.

I noticed a bit of a lilt in his voice,
  Like the note of a musical bell,
And the first thing I knew I was making a choice
  Of the things that he offered to sell.

He set me to laughing by something he said.
  What it was now I'd like to recall,
But I found when he'd gone I had needles and thread
  For which I have no use at all.

The stuff that he sold me was not what I bought
  With the small silver coin that I paid,
But the wink in his eye and the jest that he brought
  And the moment of mirth that he made.

TEA AND TOAST

Oh, time may bring troubles and time may bring
    tears,
And nobody knows what awaits down the years.
The gift of old age must be purchased with pain,
And leaving and losing the joys we may gain,
But there's always a mem'ry to cling to and keep
To balance the sorrows that cause us to weep.
So writing these few feeble verses I am
To tea and to toast and to strawberry jam.

The feasts I like best are those gay little teas
When with friends we are fond of we sit at our
    ease,
And the laughter rings out at some jest that is told
As we reach for the butter as yellow as gold.
Then our hearts and our minds from suspicion are
    free,
Shut away from the world and its heartaches are
    we,
Just good friends together, devoid of all sham,
Drinking tea, eating toast spread with strawberry
    jam.

There are some who may say that but folly is this,
That life gives us mem'ries of much greater bliss,
But I run them all over and sift them all through,
To find my joy linked to my good friends and true.
Not the feast after conquest I haste to recall,
Nor the banquet attended in some gilded hall,
But to those glad occasions I bow and salaam,
Those suppers of tea, toast and strawberry jam.

WINTER IN THE GARDEN

All that can be witnessed from my window as I
    toil
Is a white but rumpled blanket on the rose bed's
    nurturing soil
And a pine tree and a cedar which in green are
    gleaming still,
And some hardy, hungry sparrows on my narrow
    window sill.

Like a bed the boy has slept in now the ground
    appears to be,
With the blankets piled and twisted, scarcely fit for
    folks to see;
With the things he has discarded, helter-skelter
    strewn about—
Thus the garden strikes my fancy every time that
    I look out.

There's a curious sort of calmness over shrub and
    plant and vine,
And the sleeping trees stand solemn as the winds
    about them whine.
Now the song birds have departed and the lone-
    liness and gloom
Give the earth a curious likeness to a boy's deserted
    room.

(Emily Post says the father of the groom is merely another guest at the wedding. Strangers are under no obligation to speak to him.)

THE FATHER OF THE GROOM

Should you see him in the room,
In an atmosphere of gloom,
You are not obliged to say:
"Lovely wedding!" Go your way;
Hurry by to quaff the punch,
Hasten by to grab the lunch!
In his tails and fancy vest
He is just another guest—
Just the father of the groom.

If your etiquette you've learned
You don't need to feel concerned
For that lonely man who stands
Idly fumbling with his hands;
Needn't stop to ask his name;
If you snub him, none will blame.
Rights by him are not possessed.
He is just another guest—
Just the father of the groom.

This I find the case will be
In a few short months with me.
By the women I've been told
I'm the shorn lamb of the fold.
Mine's a very humble post
With no perquisites to boast,

60

So you needn't speak to me.
Just another guest I'll be—
Just the father of the groom.

❧　❧　❧

THE FATHER OF THE BRIDE

With Mrs. Emily Post as guide,
Let's view the father of the bride
And learn just what his duties are
If he would shoot the course in par.
Although the father of the groom
Within her book gets little room,
The father of the bride receives
At least a dozen printed leaves.

Since he's the man who pays the bills,
A chapter in the book he fills.
He must provide the wedding gown,
The suit for going out of town,
The dresses for the bridesmaids, too,
If that he can afford to do;
The flowers for church and home, and then
The tips for all the serving men.

The father of the bride must see
The sexton gets his usual fee.
The organist and vested choir,
The book proclaims, are his to hire.

He must arrange for men to spread
The canvas down and overhead.
Oh, yes! and he must also buy
Of linens fine a full supply.

To him, of course, the statement goes
For all the gifts the bride bestows.
The wedding feast, the wedding cake,
The pretty boxes guests will take,
The bridal pictures, wine, cigars,
The invitations, motor cars,
The orchestra which softly· plays!
For all of these her father pays.

Though no one in the crowded room
Need greet the father of the groom,
I'll say that's quite O.K. with me,
The bridegroom's dad I'm glad to be.

PLATO IN A TAXI

I walked up to a taxi, and the man who drove it sat
Deep buried in a volume—and I asked: "What book
  is that?"
It startled him to hear me, but it also startled me
When he answered: "Jowett's Plato! I enjoy philos-
  ophy."

He never saw me coming; never stirred until I
  spoke
Though the thundering waves of traffic in the city
  round him broke.
He was lost to the confusion; with a book upon his
  knees
He was back in ancient Athens at the feet of Socrates.

And I thought the while he drove me through the
  noisy city streets:
Who knows the secret yearnings of the humblest
  man he meets?
Here's an oil-stained taxi-driver hauling people to
  their gates,
P'raps to drinking bouts and revels—reading Plato
  while he waits!

Fate may play its tricks on mortals; chance the hands
  and feet may bind,
But who has the love for wisdom still is master of
  his mind.
Here's a man whose pay is meager and his task
  seems rather drab,
But Old Plato is his comrade as he drives a taxicab.

SLEIGH BELLS

In forty years we've changed the world and traded
    many things.
We've banished glowing stoves to gain the warmth
    a furnace brings.
We've polished off discomforts with invention's
    magic art.
We've built the "press the button age" when count-
    less motors start,
But thinking of my boyhood days, we lost a joy,
    I'll say,
When faithful horse and cutter were forever put
    away.
For never comes a fall of snow but what for them
    I mourn,
And that strap of tinkling sleigh bells we supplanted
    with a horn!

I would not now go back to live as once we lived
    of old,
I'm much too fond of comfort to undress in bed-
    rooms cold,
On winter nights I would not care to journey to
    the shed
And carry coal to feed the stove before I go to bed.
I'm glad such chores exist no more and I am grate-
    ful, too,
That wheeling out the ashes is a task with which
    I'm through.

I'm not the kind that loves the past and all that's
 modern scorns.
I merely say that sleigh bells were more musical
 than horns.

We give up youth for mellow age; each forward
 step we take
To reach a joy which lies ahead an old charm we
 forsake.
We deal and barter through the years old customs
 for the new;
Find easier ways to do the tasks once difficult to do,
But sometimes as we move along to build the better
 day
We learn we've been compelled to throw a lovely
 thing away.
And thinking of my boyhood days to this I will be
 sworn:
Those sleigh bells sang a prettier song than any
 motor horn.

THE BEGGAR

They mark me by the coat I wear and never glimpse
    my dreams.
They never seem to see the pain beneath these
    ragged seams.
I'm just another man to them who pass along the
    way,
Who may have had a business once but failed to
    make it pay.

They see the grime upon my face, my features
    drawn and thin,
But not the thoughts that fill my brain when night
    comes sweeping in.
Sometimes they hear the words I say and give a
    dime to me,
But that great hope I'm cherishing I know they
    never see.

They pass me by with just a glance upon my
    shabby dress.
I think they've seen too many men who've made of
    life a mess.

And so they treat us all alike and never stop to
    think
That some of us are slaves to fate and not the slaves
    to drink.

They never see the throttled pride that lumps my
    aching throat;

They only see my cold blue hand, my thin and
   tattered coat.
With "yes" or "no" they pass me by and nothing I
   can say
Convinces them how hard it is the beggar's role to
   play.

❧ ❧ ❧

CHILDHOOD

Childhood takes its hurts so lightly,
   Tears seem bitter as they fall,
But they're ended hourly, nightly.
   Life is joyous after all.

All its wrongs seem quickly mended.
   Broken toys are put away.
Quarrels come, but when they're ended
   Back the rivals run to play.

Childhood laughs away the smudges
   Tears have left upon its cheeks;
Only grownups carry grudges!
   To be happy childhood seeks.

Childhood keeps no smouldering ember
   Of the fires that blaze and burn;
Only grownups long remember
   Hurts in malice to return.

I GO HOME FOR LUNCH

In little towns I fancy still the factory whistle blows
At noon and homeward to his lunch the happy hus-
band goes,
And women folks at twelve o'clock the mid-day meal
prepare
Because their men are coming home and shortly
will be there.
I tried it out the other day, went home to lunch and
found
That city wives at noon don't care to have their
men around.

"What, home for lunch?" the mother cried. "Oh,
what a thing to do!
You know right well we haven't time to plan a
meal for you."
The maid looked startled and she said: "Give me my
coat and hat!
I don't believe I care to work where men play tricks
like that!
That means an extra place to set, an extra plate and
spoon.
Besides we've nothing in the house to feed a man at
noon."

I learned that I was wholly wrong; that times are
different now
And coming home for lunch is one thing wives do
not allow.

Two meals a day are quite enough for women folks
    to plan,
And anyhow no one at noon expects to feed a man.
So henceforth at my favorite club my mid-day meal
    I'll munch
And never bother them again by going home for
    lunch.

❧ ❧ ❧

WINTER

Winter comes to field and glen,
  And the brave youth of the spring
And the song of thrush and wren,
  And the trees gay blossoming
Fade before the cruel blast
Into glories of the past.

All things have their winter time.
  Toys lie broken with the years.
Eyes that danced with joys sublime
  Soon or late are dimmed by tears.
Youth itself becomes at last
But a memory of the past.

It is well that spring should go,
  And that summer blooms should fade;
Well that every joy we know
  Must pass onward, undelayed.
For, if pleasure could remain,
So could grief and loss and pain.

ENVY

We know not just what shadows fall
Beyond the castle wall.
We see the king ride by
But never hear his sigh.

Burdensome seem our own affairs.
We count our daily cares,
Feel them and know their weight
Is wearisome and great.

Once in a bitter envious hour
I saw a man of power
And thinking him care-free
I wished that I were he.

I would have worn his medalled coat,
The ribbon at his throat,
But not the cancer grim
Which sapped the life of him.

Envy is limited of sight,
It sees the mantle bright,
Gay plume and laurel wreath
But not the pain beneath.

PROGRESS

The old wise man put by his book
   And said: "As far as I can see,
   Adventure ends right here for me!
Beyond my day I cannot look.
   Some younger man when I have gone
   Into the dark must journey on.

"This is not all there is to know.
   With time some clearer eye shall find
   The paths to which I now am blind.
I've gone as far as I can go.
   This marks the end of my career.
   Now someone else may start from here.

"And so for him who waits behind
   I leave the sum of all I've learned,
   The bits of knowledge proved and earned
All catalogued for him to find.
   He'll start from here to build and plan
   With facts not known when I began.

"As I the benefit received
   Of all who cleared the paths for me,
   So he who follows me shall be
Of all my anxious doubts relieved.
   Thus so much farther may he go
   To learn what I can't stay to know."

THE RUNAWAY

I saw him 'neath a tropic sky
  And sad he seemed to be,
For the home-door look was in his eye,
  But he'd somehow lost the key.
He was tanned as brown as a leather shoe,
  As old and as worn and thin,
And he stood on the pier, as wanderers do,
  When the home-land ships come in.

He looked at our flag with a wistful eye,
  But smiled as we stepped ashore;
There was something weird in his "hello" cry
  Which I never had heard before.
Oh! I've heard "hello" in a thousand ways,
  But never so tinged with pain
As that greeting sad where the palm tree sways
  Down there on the Spanish Main.

"I've been going back home," he said to me,
  "Going back for years and years.
There's a place up north where I'd like to be,
  But never the chance appears.
The ships come in for a time to stay,
  But their decks to me are barred.
Oh, it's easy enough to run away,
  It's the getting back that's hard!"

Perhaps some day will a vessel stop
  For a time at that dusty town

And others may see, as the anchors drop,
   A man turned leather brown.
As they get to shore they may hear that cry,
   "Hello!" as it came to me
From him with the home-door look in his eye
   Who had somehow lost the key.

       ❧   ❧   ❧

WOMAN AND HER MIRROR

Woman is that peculiar class
Which stops before a looking glass,
And in herself sees every flaw.
Would man his faults as clearly saw!

WAKING THE BOY

At morning many a doting dad
Says: "Well, it's time to wake the lad!"
   And up the stairs he flies,
Then from that slumbrous healthy form
He jerks the covers, snug and warm
   And bids the youngster rise.

'Twas thus my father wakened me,
And thus, the task next mine to be,
   I woke that boy of mine,
And thus, so long as morn shall break,
All fathers will their youngsters wake
   At seven or eight or nine.

But yanking covers from their beds
Does little for those youthful heads
   Which locked in slumber lie.
What can we do the while they drowse
Their dormant spirits to arouse
   To rise as time goes by?

What method can we find to take
Some deep ambition to awake?
   What covers pull away
Which hold them fast and shut their eyes
Unto the golden chance that lies
   Ahead of them today?

How can we break that slumber deep
Which holds their spirits fast asleep?

What prize or golden cup
Will rouse in them the will to win,
To work, to fight through thick and thin
And really get them up?

᯾ ᯾ ᯾

THE QUITTER

Because he sulked and hung his head
When turned the battle bitter,
The spirit from his body fled.
It couldn't stand a quitter.

THE NEXT GENERATION

We shall leave you many problems; many tasks we
    couldn't do.
We shall leave a world unfinished that shall need the
    best of you,
And I wonder as I see you grouped in school and
    college still,
If you know the chance that waits you in the places
    you must fill.

The voice of opportunity is calling loud for men;
Men of wisdom, men of courage, to set right the
    world again;
Men of honor, men of vision; men the future's work
    to share;
And I wonder if you've heard it, and have started
    to prepare.

We have blundered; we have stumbled and have
    somehow lost our way.
In the wreckage of our failures we are gropers all
    today,
But you boys who follow after face a future strewn
    with need
And endless opportunities to conquer and succeed.

X-RAY PICTURES OF TWO MEN

By chance they met in the doctor's room,
  Master and workman, chair by chair;
Away from the desk and the lathe and loom
  They started to chat as they waited there.
They had quarreled long through a bitter strike,
But now they were patients, two men alike.

"What's wrong?" said one. Said the other, "Pain!
  Pain that follows my every meal!
And everything that I've tried seems vain;
  Always this burning inside I feel."
"That's queer," said the other. "I'm troubled, too,
By a similar ache like is bothering you."

The workman answered: "You must be wrong.
  You don't suffer the same as I.
Distresses like these to the poor belong.
  Whatever you need you have cash to buy."
"The X-Ray shows," said the rich man then,
"That under the skin we are just two men.

"Isn't it queer, when the films are made
  They have to number them, poor and rich,
For by nothing else that is there displayed
  Could they ever discover just which was which.
Just under the skin when the light breaks through
There is scarcely a difference twixt me and you."

VALENTINE

I'd been taking things for granted in a settled sort
of way.
Thirty years or more of marriage rub the novelty
away,
And the things you do in courtship are so easily
forgot
When life keeps its even tenor, though you think
of them or not.
We were arm in arm together, was the weather
foul or fine,
So the notion never struck me that she'd like a
valentine.

She never spoke about it. Looking back I guess she
knew
With the home and all it called for I had quite
enough to do.
There were always gifts for Christmas and an
Easter dress or hat
And a token for her birthday, so I let it go at that,
But while riding down to business I beheld a mer-
chant's sign
And somehow the notion struck me: she might like
a valentine.

So I bought a little trinket and I wrote a card to
show
It was from the foolish fellow that she married years
ago.

I had it tied with ribbons and I sent it by a boy,
But I never dreamed such nonsense could have given
   so much joy.
For she couldn't have been gladder or her eyes more
   brightly shine
Had the handsome Robert Taylor sent that valentine
   of mine.

❧　❧　❧

HONOR

Honor, with everything at stake,
Fine choice of methods still will make
And chooses, rather than to cheat
To suffer nothing but defeat.

BIG DOG

Mark is a Dane, a dog of mighty size
That wears a look of sadness in his eyes.
He grieves because he suffers many a slap
For wanting to be cuddled in your lap.
Conceived for greatness, under nature's law,
He merely wants mankind to hold his paw.
His greatest pleasure, after being fed,
Is having someone scratch his massive head.

To look at Mark you'd think he was a brute,
An animal to flee from or to shoot;
Yet he so little values strength and size
That if we speak a scolding word, he cries.
His weakness is for friendship. Round about
He runs to visit when we let him out,
And though it seems a most surprising thing
I'll swear at door bells he has learned to ring.

I think it sad a dog should be so kind
And yet so very fearfully designed
That he must miss, so long as he shall live,
The friendship that he tries so hard to give.
His bark is thunder. When he wags his tail
'Tis like the flagellation of a flail,
Yet with true greatness on his way he jogs
And leaves the snarling to the smaller dogs.

LOOKING FORWARD

There was a sage who told her
  That grief was sure to be.
He did his best to hold her
  From hurts that he could see.
He whispered: "When you marry
  You'll find the hills are steep
With many a load to carry
  And many a day to weep.

" 'Tis pain that I would spare you
  And sorrow's flood of tears.
The path where love would bear you
  Stays not as it appears.
It runs through briar and stubble
  The further on you go
There will be more of trouble
  And more of grief to know."

Said she: "That's why I marry!
  I want the right to weep.
Life's burdens I would carry.
  Life's trust I want to keep.
I look for those tomorrows
  That may be tempest-blown,
But since there must be sorrows
  I want them for my own."

ASK YOUR MOTHER

This my father often said:
  "Ask your mother."
"Do we have to go to bed?"
  "Ask your mother."
If in chorus we should cry:
"Please, a second piece of pie!"
Always this was his reply:
  "Ask your mother."

Coaxing, pleading, this we'd hear:
  "Ask your mother.
I'm not going to interfere.
  Ask your mother."
Every problem that arose
Over going out to shows
Brought from dad this solemn close:
  "Ask your mother."

Often wondered why he said:
  "Ask your mother."
Muttered o'er the book he read:
  "Ask your mother."
Used to think it strange that he
Never settled any plea,
But replied evasively:
  "Ask your mother."

Now, like him, I merely say:
  "Ask your mother."

This is much the easier way:
  "Ask your mother."
Once their pleading I denied
And it left them teary-eyed.
Now I say: "I won't decide!
  Ask your mother."

❧ ❧ ❧

REPUTATION

When champions on their laurels stay
  They soon discover to their sorrow
Fame is the crown of yesterday
  Some other man will wear tomorrow.

ETERNAL SPRING

I wonder what the world beyond can hold of beauty
    to compare
With tulips gay in early May and trees in blossom
    everywhere.
Has God some loveliness retained of bloom and bird
    for heaven alone,
Or is the fullness of His power to doubting man
    already shown?

I know beyond the bonds of flesh the souls of men
    from strife are free;
That life is ampler over there, but can the spring-
    time lovelier be?
Can breezes sweeter fragrance bear and daffodils
    more perfect grow?
Can hills and fields more splendors wear than these
    we common mortals know?

The Spring must be eternal, too. That burst of music
    in the sky
Which sings the cardinal's joy of life I cannot think
    was born to die.
I'm sure when robins nest again and beauty blos-
    soms everywhere,
Whatever else God's Heaven may hold, the Spring
    can be no lovelier there.

THE TWO SIDES

One woman sighed: "I never make
A cocoanut or chocolate cake
And put it on the pantry shelf
But what that child will help himself.

"If for an hour I'm gone from here
Always the cookies disappear.
To keep a chocolate cake for tea
I lock it up and hide the key.

"It isn't safe when I go out
To leave the candy jar about,
For every sweetmeat in the urn,
Will vanish long ere I return."

A neighbor said: "By day and night
I'm sure mine is the sadder plight.
However long I am away
Untouched my cakes and pies will stay.

"My candy jar for weeks will stand
And never know a pilfering hand.
All's safe upon my pantry shelf.
I have no child to help himself."

CHERRY PIE

I'll obey them in the winter when the doctors say
    to me
I must give up ham and spinach, and obedient
    I'll be.
To relieve my indigestion in December they can
    try,
But there's none of them can stop me when it's time
    for cherry pie.

They can shake their heads and warn me that disaster
    I shall strike
By persisting in devouring tasty victuals that I like.
I'll forego in February all the sweetmeats they deny,
But no doctor's going to stop me when it's time for
    cherry pie.

With the cherries ripe for eating and for baking I
    will take
My wedge of luscious goodness and then let the
    stomach ache.
Let the acid overpower me if it wants to, I won't cry.
There's no diet list I'll follow that would rule out
    cherry pie.

I'll be good in February. I'll do all the doctors say.
I'll eat all their tasteless victuals 'till about the end
    of May.
Then I'll turn my back upon them, and then, even
    though I die,

As I wend my way to Heaven I'll be full of cherry
    pie.

⁎ ⁎ ⁎

ALL I KNOW

Tis bitter cold for him who wears an old and
    threadbare coat.
'Tis bitter cold for him who owns no muffler for his
    throat;
And never drifts the white snow down as winter
    settles in
But what I think 'tis bitter cold for him whose shoes
    are thin.

The world is full of bickering now and full of words
    the air,
But wise men cannot talk away a poor man's bleak
    despair.
I do not know which way is best, the silver or the
    gold,
I only know who lacks a coat will find the winter
    cold.

I hear them at the tables as they argue con and
    pro,
But little of their logic do I understand or know.
I'm only sure of this as I look through the window
    pane:
It's bitter cold to trudge the streets and look for work
    in vain.

GROWING UP

Once we had a little girl, but we haven't any more,
In her place there is a lady with her skirt upon the
floor.

Once we had a little girl who wore stockings to her
knee.
Now, instead of girlish stockings, she is wearing
hosiery.

Once we had a little girl. Hand in hand we'd walk
about.
Now a dignified young woman takes my arm when
we go out.

Once we had a little girl who'd just learned her
A B C's.
She is now sophisticated, reading novels, if you
please.

Once we had a little girl and it wasn't long ago.
Now we have a charming maiden who believes she
has a beau.

Oh, these changes come so swiftly that the child
you put to bed
May wake up a grown-up lady with much wisdom
in her head.

GYPSY BLOOD

I wonder was she fair to see
Who bred the gypsy strain in me?
She lived so many years ago
Long dead are all she used to know,
And none can name the English town
To which she came and settled down,
Or tell just how she chanced to be
So far away from Romany.

My mother said she'd never heard
Of any gossip so absurd!
"You come," she said, "for ages back,
Straight forward down the Tudor track
And not a woman there appears
With golden circlets in her ears
Or any wanton, wandering maid
Who served the fortune-telling trade."

And yet with each returning spring
I get the lust for wandering,
A curious aching in the heart
With pack and tent and staff to start
And, care-free, idly wander down
To Nottingham or London town.
And how I wonder can that be
Unless there's gypsy blood in me?

THE FIRST WATCH

My father gave a watch to me
　　Long many years ago.
It was a handsome thing to see,
　　Which I was proud to show,
A bright and shining mystery
　　I was too young to know.

"Take care of it," my father said.
　　"Be sure to use it well;
Wind it before you go to bed,
　　The time of day 'twill tell."
But when possession's charm had fled,
　　A tragedy befell.

No more contented to enjoy
　　A thing so bright and fair,
I ventured as a curious boy
　　To lay its secrets bare,
Not dreaming that I should destroy
　　That watch beyond repair.

Into its gleaming case I pried,
　　Took wheels and springs apart,
But all in vain that day I tried
　　Again that watch to start.
The joy that once was mine had died
　　And left me sad at heart.

And so with man. The happiest art
　　Is blessings to accept,

For he who tears his life apart
   God's will to intercept
Will lose the blithe and joyous heart
   Which faith in Him had kept.

❧ ❧ ❧

COURTSHIPS END

I'll tell you a tale of a wee little elf
Who lived in a tulip out there by himself,
And he fell in love with my Janet when she
Was just after two and not quite up to three.

One day as I worked in the garden about
When Janet had measles and couldn't come out,
This elf of the tulip approached me and said:
"Your daughter I ask your permission to wed.

"I love her!" "Hmm-hmm," I replied, "maybe so
But my Janet is still much too young for a beau.
She's still just a baby. She hasn't turned three,
Wait twenty years longer, and then we shall see."

This happened in springtime, just ten years ago,
But that elf tired of waiting for Janet to grow.
In a fit of despair he deserted the spot
And now none of us knows if he's living or not.

MASCULINE SIGNS

When before the glass he stands,
　Plastering down each wisp of hair;
When he starts to wash his hands
　With the most surprising care;
When above his trouser belt
　He won't let his shirt unfurl,
It is plain that boy has felt
　The sweet influence of a girl.

When he keeps his fingers clean
　And his knuckles free from grime,
There's some lovely "sweet sixteen"
　That he thinks of all the time.
When he starts to fret about
　Collar points which upward curl,
There is not the slightest doubt
　That young fellow's met a girl!

When he stands with shoulders square
　And no longer lets them sag;
When his handkerchief is fair,
　Not a blackened, crumpled rag;
When he starts to brush his hat,
　Keep his teeth like gleaming pearl,
You can be assured all that
　Merely means he's met a girl!

FEMININE SIGNS

When your little girl begins
  Wanting waves put in her hair;
When the strangest sort of pins
  On her frock she starts to wear;
When the manners of the old
  Very quaintly she employs,
Plain this fact, although untold,
  She's begun to notice boys.

When expectantly she springs,
  Just as eager as can be,
Every time the phone bell rings,
  Saying: "That may be for me!"
When the chatter endless flows
  Till it irks you and annoys,
That's another sign which shows
  She's begun to notice boys.

When she begs a drop of scent
  And the powder which you use;
When no longer she's content
  With those healthy, flat-heeled shoes;
When she starts to think about
  Losing weight and gaining poise,
Then there isn't any doubt
  She's begun to notice boys.

DOG TRAINER

Bill could take a puppy and teach him clever tricks.
He would spend an afternoon sending him for
sticks;
Patient with him as he could be; kind and gentle,
too,
Till he'd made him understand what he had to do.
Bill could raise the kind of dog everyone enjoys.
Oft I wished that Bill had been as patient with his
boys.

Catch a puppy chewing things, Bill would merely
smile.
"He'll get over that," he'd say, "in a little while.
That's the nature of the beast. Give him time to
grow.
What is right and what is wrong pretty soon he'll
know."
Understood the ways of dogs; all their habits knew.
But he couldn't teach his boys what they ought
to do.

Bill had time to train a dog. That to him was fun,
But somehow he never learned how to train a son;
When they blundered into wrong such a fuss he
made
That of him his youngsters were constantly afraid.
"Dogs need patience," oft he said, "if you'd have 'em
good."

But that boys need patience, too, Bill never understood.

Bill's boys never came to much; soon they both
    cleared out.
They grew up to be the sort no one likes about.
Pity, too, I've often thought. Bill a dog could train,
But to boys the way to act he never could explain.
Still I'm sure to better men they'd have both grown
    up
Had he given them half the time spent upon a pup.

❧   ❧   ❧

BEAUTY

The lovely things museums hold
Are beauty frozen in a mold,
But so much lovelier to the eye
Are living charms that fade and die.

THE MOTHERS AT THE WINDOWS

They sit beside the windows when the sun is slip-
    ping down,
Just watching for their men-folk who are coming
    from the town.
The home is clean and tidy and the supper table's
    spread,
And soon they'll turn the corner—hungry men who
    must be fed.

Day by day at evening at the windows you can see
The eager mothers watching, as they watched for
    you and me.
The sons have started working. They are sturdy,
    stalwart men.
It is drawing on to night time and they're coming
    home again.

They glory in the stories that their men-folk have
    to tell.
They can read it in their faces when the day has
    ended well.
They are always at the windows, world-wide over
    though you roam,
The patient mothers watching for their men-folk
    coming home.

LITTLE BY LITTLE

Inch by inch and a foot is gained.
  Two feet more and a yard is made.
Little by little is much attained.
  Ounce by ounce and a pound is weighed.
Day by day and a week has passed.
  Four full weeks and a month has flown.
Twelve brief months and we find at last
  Out of them all a year has grown.

A day seems long and a mile seems far
  And you scarcely notice the yard you've gained,
But by that much nearer the goal posts are,
  And nearer still when the mile's attained.
Oh, the hills seem steep when you start to climb,
  But upward struggle and don't you stop,
As the acorn grows to an oak in time,
  Little by little you'll reach the top.

Ounce by ounce and a pound is weighed,
  And by and by are the pounds a ton;
Though swift or slow was the progress made,
  It is all the same when the goal is won.
For whether you leap or whether you crawl,
  You'll find this truth—and it's ages old!
That success is merely the sum of all
  The tedious inches in miles retold.

LITTLE BATTERED LEGS GROWS UP

I chuckle as I see her in her pretty party dress
With a ribbon made to match it, tied about a single
tress.
I chuckle and I wonder if that maiden that I see
Is the little girl last summer who so boyish seemed
to be.

She walks so very stately and so quickly time has
flown
That I can't believe this lady is the child I used to
own.
Now I see a long gown trailing and I marvel at her
charms.
Are those her mother's bracelets she is wearing on
her arms?

Is that the child, I wonder, who so often scampered
in
With her legs all cuts and bruises which we smeared
with iodine?
Can this very lovely maiden, now the daintiest of
sights,
Be the one whose legs, last summer, were a mass of
"skeeter bites?"

Just a step from "rough and tumble" into "loveliness
and charm;"
Just a step from cuts and bruises, to a bracelet on
her arm!

Now she's blossomed into girlhood and I think it
    safe to say
We can put that little bottle filled with iodine away.

❧   ❧   ❧

MAN'S NAME

Man's name is that tenacious thing
To which all faults and graces cling.

Attached to it, for all to see,
Is everything he's dared to be.

His manners, habits, thoughts and airs
Are stamped upon the name he bears.

It is the scroll on which he writes
His loves, his hatreds and delights.

'Tis not by common flesh and bone,
But by his name a man is known,

For all his failures and his gains
His name tenaciously retains.

THE GULLIBLE FISHERMEN

At Silver Lake three fishermen got up at break of
    day
To go for bass in Maiden Lake, just forty miles
    away.
"We'll get 'em there!" one angler said, "beyond the
    slightest doubt.
For that's a place for small mouthed bass not many
    know about."

So bag and baggage off they went to fish that secret
    spot
Which strangely in this crowded world shared not
    the common lot.
It nestled forty miles away. The guide had pledged
    his word
That only he and one or two of Maiden Lake had
    heard.

That self-same morn at Maiden Lake three fisher-
    men arose
And dressed in silence, not to break their comrades'
    sweet repose.
They started off for Silver Lake, where monsters
    could be hooked;
A paradise for anglers which the crowd had over-
    looked.

Twixt Maiden Lake and Silver Lake these brothers
    chanced to meet.

"Don't tell 'em where we're going!" said the guides
  who were discreet.
So six mysterious fishermen changed places for the
  day
And the guides winked at each other as they went
  upon their way.

❧ ❧ ❧

EULOGY

This was the way of him, minister, say of him
  Only the simplest of praises about him,
Flatter him not today, it is enough to say
  Care will be just a bit harder without him.

Friend to us all was he, soonest to call was he
  Hearing the word that our hearts were in sorrow;
This is enough to say, now that he's gone away:
  Grief will be just a bit harder tomorrow.

Now that he's gone away, we who still living stay,
  Missing his smile and his hand at our shoulder,
As the days come and go, 'gainst all the storms that
  blow
  Stronger will have to be, truer and bolder.

PACK PEDDLER

He took his pack upon his back
  And lugged it round all day.
Where people dwell he went to sell
  Or oft be turned away.
"A creature grim!" some said of him,
  "A sorry sight to see!"
Some merely thought of what they bought
  And what its cost would be.

Not one inquired if he were tired
  Or were his youngsters well;
None asked his name or how he came
  Such trifling things to sell.
With "will it wear?" they'd stop and stare
  At every pot and pan,
The tiniest flaw in tin they saw,
  Who never saw the man!

The barter done he journeyed on
  But where nobody knew;
  A peddler, he, they'd never see
  When once he passed from view.
Yet strange it seems, men shape their dreams
  And work by devious plans;
Some play the saint; some write; some paint;
  Some peddle pots and pans.

TALK OVER THERE

There will be much to talk about,
  We who are late in leaving
Shall some day yonder seek them out
  And, done with all our grieving,
We'll settle down, no more to roam,
And give them all the news of home.

There will be much for us to tell,
  So long on earth we've tarried.
They'll want to know who's doing well
  And who has lately married
And do we still keep Christmas Day
And birthdays in the same old way?

What of the neighbors on the street?
  I fancy them inquiring,
How often does the family meet?
  Are mortals still desiring
Only the joys of life to know
And never doubt or care or woe?

I know the questions thick and fast
  Around us will be flying:
How did you manage at the last?
  Were you afraid of dying?
Well, all your fears have come to naught.
You found it easier than you thought.

DAD DISCUSSES CLOTHES

Mother wants a party dress.
  Janet wants one, too;
So, old pants o' mine, I guess
  You will have to do.
Just a little shiny now,
  Baggy at the knee.
What's the difference anyhow?
  No one looks at me.

I can wait a little while.
  What's a patch or two?
I don't have to be in style
  As the women do.
And a little party dress
  Prettier would be,
Meaning more of happiness
  Than would pants for me.

Rather hear the women say,
  "My, how nice you look!"
When the mother's on display,
  "Like a picture book."
Hearing such a compliment
  Prouder would I be
Than to have the money spent
  On a suit for me.

Wouldn't want it otherwise!
  Want 'em fair to see.

Every gown my money buys
  Happier makes me.
Now she wants another dress,
  Janet needs one, too,
So, old pants o' mine, I guess
  You will have to do.

❧　❧　❧

KNOWLEDGE AND DOUBT

The wise know much; they know what not to try.
They know the hazards where the dangers lie.
They know the stopping places; where to stay;
They know the books, as printed yesterday,
But past the wise the dreamer dares to go,
Tomorrow is the land he wants to know.

The wise are cautious. They would be secure.
They seldom walk a pathway till they're sure.
The books say: "No! Past this no man has gone!"
Some doubter thinks the truth lies farther on.
He dares to leap the barriers alone
And finds a fact the wise had never known.

Not from the wise but from the daring mind
Comes progress, since the wise men stay behind.
The sages know the limits all too well.
Only what now is possible they tell,
But some brave doubter o'er the barrier looks
And finds a truth not printed in the books.

MAN

I would not play it the hog's way
Or even the dog's way.
I would sit calmly and eat
My bread and my meat.
I would not sprawl on the floor
  Nor splash in the trough to get all,
Seeking the last drop and more.
  Nor in the dirt would I crawl,
Rooting the mud with my snout
For the crumbs I could well do without.

Two-legged, upright, God made me!
And this compliment paid me:
Others by instinct are bound.
Wolf, hog and hound
Must look to themselves to the end,
  But from instinct's command you are free!
You can be neighbor and friend;
  Can be what you've courage to be!
You can think and can dream and can plan,
For you have the role of a man!

And if I should play it the hog's way
Or even the dog's way,
The snarl and the grunt
Would my reason affront.
Still to scramble and struggle for more,
  Still to think I had naught I could spare
If there should come a tap on my door

To the friend or the stranger out there
Would be to stop short of the plan
Which God had in mind for a man.

❧ ❧ ❧

WHAT MATTERS IT?

What matters it when I have dined
   On meat and cherry pie
That richer men themselves have lined
   With costlier food than I?

What matters it when blows the storm
   If stout the coat I wear,
Am I not just as snug and warm
   As is the millionaire?

If all night long in slumber deep
   Upon my bed I lie,
Can rich men any sounder sleep
   Or happier wake, than I?

And since both rich and poor must die,
   When comes the day of doom,
What matters where the dead must lie,
   Grass mound or marble tomb?

COURTESY ON DEPARTURE

To host and hostess at the door,
  Handshaking as we go,
'Tis courtesy to say once more
  What they must surely know:
"Good-bye! It was so good of you.
  Your party was sublime!
We've both enjoyed the evening through.
  We've had a glorious time!"

We stay a moment in the hall
  Before we take the road
To thank our gracious friends for all
  The pleasure they've bestowed,
And as we turn to go away
  We hear the stair clock chime.
"Good-bye! Good-bye!" again we say.
  "We've had a glorious time!"

So from the host that's known as Life
  When I at last depart,
Forgetting all the care and strife
  And every sting and smart,
Let me in that last hour ere I
  Set out for realms sublime,
Shake hands with life and say: "Good-bye!
  I've had a glorious time."

STREET SCENE

I walked a little street at night,
  Past houses in a row,
And some were dark and some were light,
  The parlors still aglow,
And that is why today I write
  Of folks I do not know.

Beneath a lamp a woman sat.
  What book was that she read?
She waited (I was sure of that)
  Someone's familiar tread.
A laughing group near by was at
  A table breaking bread.

Then startled by a flood of light,
  As wide a doorway went,
For just a moment I caught sight
  Of one on business bent;
A doctor summoned in the night!
  And knew just what that meant.

Not far away a party gay
  Was shouting loud goodbyes;
I thought: In one at cards they play;
  Next door a neighbor dies;
Thus life is lived from day to day
  By foolish men and wise.

THE DOCTOR'S FIRST QUERY

When comes my doctor unto me
  In answer to my pleading,
To give that balm for agony
  Which I am sorely needing,
When he has put his coat away
  And made his formal greeting,
He'll look at me and sternly say:
  "Well, what have you been eating?"

As like a timid child I rise
  To tell my tale of anguish,
How spots are thick before my eyes
  As I in fever languish.
He shakes his wise old head and gray
  At all that I'm repeating;
Then to the good wife turns to say:
  "Well, what has he been eating?"

Is there no other source of pain
  Than pie and cake and cheeses,
Do I from red roast beef obtain
  Whatever my disease is?
Is there no way, in innocence,
  Of stray bacilli meeting
That always he must thus commence:
  "Well, what have you been eating?"

If to that far-off Heavenly shore
  My doctor goes before me,

And standing at the pearly door
  I find him waiting for me,
I'll wager as I step inside
  Where angel wings are beating,
He'll say to me: "And so you've died!
  Well, what had you been eating?"

❧ ❧ ❧

COLUMBUS

He had no light nor printed chart
  Nor sign by which to go.
He only cherished in his heart
  The faith it would be so.

The wisest scoffed and cried him "nay"
  In scorn their lips were curled,
But still he dared to sail away
  And find another world.

He dared to pass beyond the rim
  Of knowledge proved and tried,
Where faith alone could counsel him
  And faith alone could guide.

And still men hear the cautious "No"
  And heed the boastful wise,
Refusing faith which bids them go
  Where high adventure lies.

THOSE CANDID PICTURES

Time was when you had to look
Slick to have your picture took;
Women dressed you up and spent
Hours on you before you went
To the photo fellow's place;
Made you shave and scrub your face;
Plaster down your hair and throw
Back your coat so you could show
Stretched across your vest and plain
Your Masonic charm and chain.
Then the bulb was never pressed
Till you looked your very best.

Then the camera fellow stood
Eyeing you, as if he could
Change your face. He'd fix your tie,
Prop your head and chin up high;
Tug your vest and press it down;
Tell you not to wear a frown
And he'd rest and wait awhile
Till he caught you with a smile.
Then he sold you cabinets small,
And a "life-sized" for the wall
You could be remembered by
Should you ever come to die.

Now these candid fellows take
Pictures of you eating cake,
Coughing, sneezing, and you look

Like you were some wanted crook.
They sneak on you unaware;
When you haven't brushed your hair;
When you're scratching of your head
Thinking over what's been said.
I remember there was one
Took me with my old clothes on
Working in the garden. He
Said that's how he wanted me!

At your best they took you first,
Now they get you at your worst.

❧ ❧ ❧

THE MASTER

He never thought it stepping down
  To walk with men who earned their bread
Their joys and woes to share He chose,
  He understood the tears they shed.

CLUB PRESIDENTS

I've never been a president and what I write today
Is merely what I've witnessed in an unofficial way.
In the clubs that I belong to every president I've
   known
Has to bear the members' worries in addition to his
   own.

They write him endless letters telling him just what
   is wrong.
The water is too hot or cold; the tea too weak or
   strong;
The apple pies are soggy and the steaks and chops
   are tough;
The medium rare is overdone; the well done, not
   enough.

They wait for him in corners; when at dinner he
   appears
Some complaining fellow member has a grievance
   for his ears.
A few are being favored and the president should
   know
Some get the choicest tables for the tips which they
   bestow.

From the day that he's elected to the ending of his
   year
The wailing of his fellows is the only sound he'll
   hear.

Even friends will turn upon him when some trifle
    goes awry,
Yet men seem to want the office—and I often won-
    der why.

❀   ❀   ❀

"I WANT TO BETTER MYSELF!"

"I want to better myself," he said.
The commonest thought in a youngster's head.

"I want to get out of the place I'm in
To another field where there's more to win."

"Sit down," said the boss, "and I'll tell you how
You can better yourself where you are right now.

"Stop watching the clock; give thought to your task.
Do just a bit more than your chief would ask;

"If you really mean what I've heard you say,
That you'd better yourself, you can start today.

"But to change your job for a bit more pay
Won't help you much if unchanged you stay.

"For here is a truth that all should learn:
The better men labor, the more they earn.

"If it's better money that you'd enjoy,
You first must better yourself, my boy."

INCIDENT AT BETHLEHEM

Long years ago he looked at her and sadly shook
his head.
"We soon must go to Bethlehem to register," he
said.
And Mary smiled at Joseph, " 'Twill be difficult,"
said she,
But the Lord has made a promise that no harm shall
come to me."

She trudged along the highway as her time of travail
neared.
She heard the inn was crowded when at Bethlehem
they appeared.
And then she said to Joseph, "In the stable it must
be!
But the Lord has made a promise that no harm
shall come to me."

Soon the shepherds came to Mary; they had heard
the news afar.
To the Prince of Peace, they told her they'd been
guided by a star!
They adored her new born baby! Oh how strangely
things occur!
And the Lord had kept His promise that no harm
should come to her.

THE FLORIST'S STORY

Some telephone for orchids, and they never ask the
cost.
Some toss them in the rubbish when the first pink
blush is lost.
Some purchase them in clusters and their charm is
quickly gone,
But I know they've worked to get it when I sell them
only one.

He was cold and he looked hungry and he seemed
almost afraid
As I counted o'er the quarters and the nickels which
he paid.
"Shall I send it, sir?" I asked him. "No, I'll take
it now," he said,
"It's a present for a lady who is lying sick-a-bed."

"She has seen 'em in the windows and on many a
pretty dress.
We've walked by here to admire 'em. It's her fa-
vorite flower I guess!
For the pretty things she's wanted all her life she
couldn't pay,
And she's never had an orchid, but she's getting one
today!"

RIPE OLD AGE

"If to a ripe old age you'd live
Then heed these warnings that I give,"
The doctor said: "Drop every care
And every burden that you bear.
Be not disturbed by loss or gain,
View all things with supreme disdain.
Dismiss at once both love and hate
And like a cabbage vegetate."

"A ripe old age!" As there I sat
I wondered what is meant by that.
Summed up in terms of useful years
Commendable the goal appears,
But homeward bound I chanced to see
Within a yard an apple tree
Stripped bare of every fruit, but one
Which hung the topmost branch upon.

Still to the leafless twig it clung
A withered thing that once was young;
It had outlived its brothers all;
Had seen companions early fall.
It had escaped the storms and missed
The hungry youngster's eager fist.
Too high for men to reach or climb
It had eluded harvest time.

"A ripe old age!" I shook my head
Recalling what the doctor said.

Away from care and worry run
And every useful purpose shun.
"A ripe old age!" It sounded nice!
I wondered is it worth the price?
Does any man desire to be
The oldest apple on the tree?

❧   ❧   ❧

DREAMS

Men mould their lives as potters mould their clay.
Unworked, the clod a sullen clod will stay.
Chance never has, I think, and never will
Produce a thing of beauty or of skill.

Life is the raw stuff given to man and beast.
The lowest creatures work with it the least.
The only arts they strive to gain are those
Required for finding food and braving foes.

Man shapes his mass of life to suit his will;
Wants something more than food his mouth to fill.
Merely to live is not enough! He tries
Above the dreary commonplace to rise.

Men mould their years in much the self-same way
The potter fashions beauty out of clay;
With life itself the beast contented seems,
But men become the product of their dreams.

WHEN I SING

When I was but a youngster small
  The music teacher said,
"I think you needn't sing at all,
  Just read the words instead.
I've never known a little boy
  So deaf to tone to be,
Who sang with such a burst of joy
  But always off the key."

My mother labored patiently
  At the piano keys,
Determined she would teach to me
  Those simple "do-re-mi's."
But o'er her face a frown would fall
  At every note she'd strike.
She'd say: "It is no use at all!
  You sing them all alike."

When Nellie I began to woo
  By deep devotion swayed,
I sang, as ardent lovers do
  An evening serenade.
But oh, it cut me to the quick
  To hear her father shout:
"If that's the cat that's taken sick
  I wish you'd put him out."

I have the frenzy for the phrase
  As often I have shown,

The heart for singing roundelays,
　I only lack the tone.
But now my children, truth to tell,
　Think it the clever thing
To ask me if I'm feeling well
　When I begin to sing.

❧　❧　❧

THE LONELY MAN

I wish that I could think of something comforting
　to say.
I wish I felt that words of mine could take his grief
　away.
He looks so sad and lonely and the pain is all so
　plain.
It seems useless now to tell him that he'll some day
　smile again.
They've been forty years together! Now he's sitting
　there alone
And everywhere he turns to look he sees her
　shadow thrown.

I can think of things to tell him when I'm going to
　pay a call;
Some pretty speech to cheer him, but to meet him
　in the hall
Where they always stood together when their friends
　were at the door,

And to see him there without her, makes me hesi-
tate once more;
For I fancy that he called her when he heard the
door bell ring,
Since that always was his habit—and to habit man
will cling.

They've put away her pictures! What's the sense of
doing that
When before him every minute is the chair in which
she sat?
They changed the rooms a little—made them dif-
ferent than they were—
But everything about him is reminding him of her!
Forty years they lived together! Oh, I cannot say it
yet!
He would think I'd lost my senses should I urge
him to forget.

SOME OTHER TIME

She says: "Tonight, let's call on friends!" and I,
Eager to rest, "Some other time!" reply.
"They've had a spell of sickness there, I know,
But I should have to shave if we should go.
Stay home tonight. To bed we'll early climb,
We'll make that visit at 'some other time.'"

"Write them a letter," mother says, and I,
Deep in a book, "Some other time," reply.
"The paper isn't handy and I think
My fountain pen's entirely out of ink.
I want to solve this most mysterious crime!
I'll get that letter off 'some other time.'"

Some other time! The letter's never penned!
Some other time! Too late to cheer a friend!
And all because at home we choose to stay
Rather than change our dress to go away.
"Now," says the clock, as it begins to chime.
"Not now!" we answer, "but 'some other time.'"

In many ways men nobly will behave,
But still begrudge the time it takes to shave!
Since pen and paper lie ten steps away,
Unwritten, countless hoped-for letters stay.
"Some other time," we cry, as if, somehow,
"Some other time" could better be than now.

I VOLUNTEER

Last night the mother said to me:
"Well, what about a Christmas tree?"
　And "what about it?" I inquired,
　　Not guessing what was on her mind.
　　"Of Christmas trees have you grown tired?
　　Have we left all those joys behind?"
"Oh no!" she said, but still this year
There is no need to have one here.

"You see," and then she faintly smiled,
"We haven't any little child.
　Janet has put her dolls away,
　　A grown young lady now, and so
　I thought for her this Christmas Day
　　To hang a bough of mistletoe.
We're all too old, it seemed to me
To bother with a Christmas tree."

I stirred the sugar in my cup.
"That's right," I said, "we've all grown up!
　No little boy or girl have we.
　　To that we both are reconciled,
　But we should have a Christmas tree
　　So this year I will be a child.
We've got to keep the old-time joy.
I'll be this household's little boy!

"I'm grown, but not too grown for things
Of rapture which the Christmas brings!

If it's a child you want about
  I'll guarantee to fill the bill.
As gayly round the place I'll shout
  As any happy youngster will.
You've got a little boy in me
Who wants to have a Christmas tree!"

＊　＊　＊

BOARDING THE BIRDS

I run a boarding house all winter long
  For quail and pheasant and the sturdy sparrow.
The pay I ask is just a bit of song
  And, lest this life of mine shall grow too narrow,
A glimpse of something different now and then
From cold, bleak highways peopled thick with men

At dinner time come in the hungry birds
  To find the corn spread out as on a platter;
They tell me nothing in so many words.
  They eat and leave without a lot of chatter.
Yet that white ring around the pheasant's neck
Is quite enough to pay the dinner check.

Sometimes I think how bare this life would be
  If never song bird happened by to cheer us
If, being human, ostracized were we
  By every other creature living near us.
We'd get along somehow beyond a doubt!
It's pleasanter to have the birds about.

NEW METHOD OF THINKING

"Yes," he said, "I hear you grumbling at the loads
    you have to bear.
They look big and mighty heavy through the glasses
    of despair.
You remember all your troubles; you can count
    them one and all,
But the blessings showered upon you very seldom
    you recall.
Now your lives would all be brighter from the start
    unto the close
If you'd magnify your pleasures as you magnify
    your woes.

"Oh, you sisters! Oh, you brothers! I'm no learned
    preacher man,
But I know the good Lord wants us just to do the
    best we can.
Here you walk about His garden and His flowers
    you fail to see,
Since your eyes are always looking for some fault
    which shouldn't be.
You've got twisted in your vision and you ought to
    set it straight.
You see every pleasure little and see every trouble
    great.

"With a grateful heart make bigger every joy on you
    bestowed!

If your way be long and weary count the flowers
    beside the road.
You make records of your troubles. Those you'll
    multiply and add,
But there's none of you subtracting from their sum
    the joys you've had.
So here's a better method, which I venture to pro-
    pose,
Which is magnify your blessings as you magnify
    your woes."

         ❧   ❧   ❧

NOT A MAN'S JOB

It's getting on to Christmas and the days drag
    slowly by
For the youngsters who are waiting, but for us they
    fairly fly.
These are busy times for mother while she's work-
    ing on her list
Making careful preparation so that no one shall be
    missed.
And I chuckle as I watch her, for I wonder now
    and then
What we'd find on Christmas morning if they left
    it to the men.

Oh, I don't know how to say it, now the bustling
    starts anew,
But this work of preparation is a job no man could
    do.

Even Sampson would have shirked it. Chasing
round from store to store
Would have left him sad and weary. And I think
of something more.
There'd be many folks forgotten when the Christmas
morn began
If the plans and preparations all depended on a
man.

It needs women folk to run it and I'm grateful that
they will.
If they'll only do the shopping I'll be glad to pay
the bill.
For the loving and the laughter that the Christmas
day will bring
From the hearts of all the women and their deep
devotion spring.
Now the shopping season's with us and they're at it
once again!
But 'twould never seem like Christmas if they left
it to the men.

THE HUMBLE THRONG

The struggle is ever for gold and fame,
The higher inch for the world's acclaim,
The swiftest mile and the boldest deed,
As if these were all of the world's great need.
And the players play and the fighters fight
For the few brief lines which the critics write,
While the humbler toilers must find content
On the narrower streets where their lives are spent.

Out of the dim dark past there comes
The far-off rumble of warriors' drums,
And the world still bears on its troubled breast
The crumbling signs of a bygone best;
But little is left of the but and ben
Which sheltered the hopes of all humbler men,
Or the tender mothers who watched and prayed
And guarded the ground where their babies played.

No doubt they found, as we, too, must do,
Their joys in the dreams which we all pursue.
Heedless of critics and mindless of fame,
They lived, loved, laughed till the last day came;
Neighbored, were kindly, suffered and wept,
And something of faith in their hearts they kept,
And found the true peace which we all desire
In the happy hours at their own hearth fire.

BEST OF ALL MEALS

I've sat at banquet tables with the greatest of the
land.
I've done my share of eating to the music of a band.
I've fed on railway diners and on rich men's yachts
at sea;
From coast to coast I've eaten wheresoe'er I chanced
to be
But the finest meal I know of, and I say it with a
grin,
Is that Sunday evening supper when our friends
drop in.

You can have your decorations, your balloons and
paper caps;
You can have your breast of guinea and your chicken
legs in wraps.
They are good for celebrations, but the festive atmos-
phere
Loses something when you face it more than once
or twice a year.
So, for regular enjoyment I will take that merry din
Of the Sunday evening supper when our friends
drop in.

You can have your bland headwaiter with his hand
held out for tips,
As for me, I vote for mother with the smile upon
her lips
And the girls out in the kitchen through the ice box
on the prowl,

Finding everything from pudding up to cold left-
over fowl.
When you get to talking victuals there's no meal
such praise can win
As that good old Sunday supper when our friends
drop in.

❧ ❧ ❧

A BOOKKEEPER'S SON

My father wrote in ledgers and he dealt with figures
cold,
His debits and his credits always balanced, so I'm
told,
He totaled lengthy columns with the rapid speed of
light,
And the sums that he arrived at always were exactly
right!
Now I must be like my mother, for as far as I can
see
My father's knack at figures wasn't handed down
to me.

I can't add a list of numbers and be sure that I'm
correct.
The answer's always different from the one that I
expect;
When I make the upward journey and at ninety I
arrive

Coming down the self-same column all I get is
eighty-five.
And I find it most confusing when again the task
I do
To discover that my total then has grown to ninety-
two.

With a single set of figures I could labor all day
long
And get forty different answers and I'm sure they'd
all be wrong;
For like little imps and demons never still the num-
bers stay
And at me they thumb their noses in a most offensive
way.
They keep dancing off the pages when in line they
ought to be,
Since my father's knack at figures wasn't handed
down to me.

PERMANENT

Those who worshiped Mammon by Mammon were
    betrayed,
For gone are all his golden coins and all the friend-
    ships made.
And now they walk in loneliness and desolate are
    they,
For everything which Mammon gave the storms
    have swept away.

But those who kept their faith alive their faith today
    possess;
And those who gloried in their friends still find
    their love no less.
And those who built their dreams around the simple
    joys of old
Still know the warmth of brotherhood although the
    winds blow cold.

These things there are which never change — the
    tulips in the spring,
The beauty of a friendly deed, the song the robins
    sing.
The glory of abiding faith, whose joys of these are
    made,
May face whatever comes without the fear of being
    betrayed.

MEMORY

It didn't seem important when it happened years
    ago.
It was just a passing pleasure like a lot we used to
    know.
We were young and life was joyous and we took it
    on the wing,
And we'd not the slightest notion of the worth of
    such a thing.
But today we're looking backwards and our mem-
    ories we find
Through all that since has happened have been
    keeping that in mind.

It was just a simple gathering. One you'd never
    guess at all
To have anything about it that you'd later on recall,
But last night we lived it over and remembered
    what was said
And there's seven of us living and the others now
    are dead.
Why we'd even kept the laughter and the jests with-
    out a change!
They'd outlasted greater glories, and I think that's
    rather strange.

'Twas a pleasure passed unnoticed. If the choice
    had been our own
It would long have been forgotten. But man's
    memory works alone

And it never asks for counsel, never questions us
    at all
If we think the fleeting moment one worth keep-
    ing to recall.
And the strangest thing about it, is that after all the
    years
When we find it's been remembered how important
    it appears!

❧ ❧ ❧

THEY DIDN'T KNOW

They only knew her garden was a pretty spot to
    see.
They only knew that day by day out there she
    seemed to be.
But just what she was doing when the roses used
    to grow
They never thought to ask her as they saw her
    come and go.

They knew that she was busy in her garden day by
    day
And always in the summer she had flowers to give
    away;
But they thought, once being planted, all unaided
    blossoms grew,
And the care that roses ask for was a thing they
    never knew.

Now that garden once so lovely lacks her wise de-
    voted care,

And the roses are not blooming as they did when
  she was there.
There are tall canes, wild and thorny left to flourish
  and to sprout
Which the mother, were she living, would have
  quickly taken out.

Now they wonder why her garden is no longer
  fair to see;
Why there's scarce a rose in blossom where profusion
  used to be,
But so often ruin follows when the happy gardeners
  go
There's so much about a garden that you really have
  to know.

❧   ❧   ❧

HAND-PAINTED CHINA DAYS

In the days of long ago every lady had to know
  How to paint a bunch of pansies on each saucer,
  cup and plate.
And a butter dish where grew no pink rosebud
  wouldn't do
  Since the fashion called for china most peculiarly
  ornate.

I wonder if at all those lost splendors you recall
  When the stuff they called "hand-painted" was
  the very smartest thing;

When the plainest gravy boat had carnations at its
    throat,
  And every dish of spinach wore the violets of
    spring.

Plates and cups were edged with gold, just as thick
    as they could hold,
  And we stared at purple pansies as we bent to
    cool our soup;
Then the crocus used to flash through the steaming
    corned beef hash,
  And beneath the mashed potatoes bloomed a lovely
    floral group.

But today nobody spills salt from fields of daffodils,
  And the ham and eggs no longer rest on beds of
    asphodel.
Where the greasy pork chops lie, not one blossom
    greets the eye.
  Those "hand-painted" days have have vanished
    and I think it's just as well.

THE MAN WHO IS GOOD TO A BOY

The man who is good to a boy may forget
  And think of that youngster no more.
He may die on the gallows for murder, and yet
  That boy, till life's journey is o'er,
Will wonder about him and keep him in mind,
And think him a hero because he was kind.

The man who is good to a boy may pass on
  And never once think of the lad,
But the boy will remember long after he's gone
  The wonderful friend he once had.
And down through the years of his life he'll recall
With affection that kindly and first friend of all.

What makes me think such a fancy is true?
  Well, a graybeard was chatting today
And he told me how often he'd wished that he knew
  Where his first friend had vanished away.
He seemed to him then, and he thinks of him yet,
As the handsomest man that he ever has met.

"He may have gone up or he may have gone down
  And today he is dead beyond doubt,
But with me he lives on with a lasting renown
  That nothing can ever wash out.
I remember him still with the greatest of joy
That man who passed by and was good to a boy."

THE KING

The King rode out through the palace gate,
Where hand in hand stood Harry and Kate,
And Harry said, touching his bowler's brim,
" 'Ere comes the King! Long life to him!"

" 'Ark to the cheers as 'e rides along!
A fine brave sight to that 'appy throng.
To the end of our days the greatest thing
We shall 'ave to boast is we've seen the king.

" 'E's the big event of our 'oliday!
'E's the 'ead and front of the world's display!
'E's the proudest memory we'll recall
And some day tell to our children small.

"But the king can't ride on a ha'p'ny bus
Nor share in the fun that belongs to us;
And he can't know what it means to wait
For a look at the king at the palace gate.

"For 'e's the king, and 'e's the show;
Wherever 'e journeys 'is guards must go!
An' 'e'll never know till 'e comes to die
The thrill of seeing the king go by."

THANKSGIVING DAY

"We are the old folks now," said I, "How fast time
    slips away!
For years we were the children coming home
    Thanksgiving Day,
But now it's ours to give the feast and stretch the
    table out
And hire an extra girl to come and pass the food
    about.
How glad they were, your folks and mine, when
    with them all could be.
Well, here it is Thanksgiving Day! The old folks
    now are we!

"They're coming home as once we did to keep
    Thanksgiving Day.
We never dreamed the weeks were long until they
    went away.
We never guessed the joy it meant to have them all
    again
About the table as of old. We were the children
    then.
But we're the old folks now, my dear, making the
    self-same fuss
Because the youngsters will be here to spend the
    day with us.

"We've bought turkey for the feast and all the trim-
    mings, too;
We'll load the table till it groans as our folks used
    to do;

I'll have to do the carving now, but when they're
all in place
I'll wait until we've bowed our heads and said the
old-time grace.
The one they taught us years ago and always used
to say
With all the family gathered round upon Thanks-
giving Day.

"Do you recall those good old times? We thought
they'd never change.
We sometimes saw a falling tear, and fancied that
was strange.
We felt the welcome hugs they gave when home to
them we went,
But never really understood just what those visits
meant.
Today we know about it all, and as our heads we
bow,
We'll think of them whose chairs we fill, for we're
the old folks now."

BOYHOOD AMBITIONS

When I was just a little lad it really seemed to me
A helmeted policeman I should like to grow to be,
That coat with shiny buttons was a dress I longed
　　to wear
And regulate the traffic on some busy thoroughfare.
But all the dreams of boyhood seem to change from
　　day to day.
My next choice was the postman in his uniform of
　　gray.

One very chilly morning we were roused in scant
　　attire.
The cause of the excitement was a neighbor's house
　　on fire.
The blaze was unimportant, but it greatly altered me.
A hook and ladder driver I determined then to be;
But I found I thought it better, at the early age of
　　four,
To run the elevator in a big department store.

One very pleasant summer I was taken on a trip
And gained a new ambition to be captain of a ship.
But later at a circus I was seized with the desire
To wear a cape of silver and do stunts upon a wire.
I caught the cowboy fever and in dreams I used to
　　go
Across the plains sky-hootin' after herds of buffalo.

Oh, you postmen and policemen and you firemen
　　rushing by,

I wonder are you conscious of the dreams that you
    supply.
Though at times you grow aweary of the tasks you
    daily meet,
Don't you sense the admiration of the children on
    the street?
Is it not a satisfaction—oft this thought occurs to
    me—
To know you're being something that all youngsters
    long to be?

      ❧   ❧   ❧

ABSENCE

I should be busy about the place
And trimming the windows again with lace.
I should be weaving a rug for the floor,
But what is the use since he'll come no more.

It is evening now and I ought to be
Getting the things that he liked for tea;
But I dread to have supper-time draw near
For it only reminds me he won't be here.

I sweep the floors as a dull routine,
But what do they matter now, soiled or clean?
And here I am still with an old dress on,
For he that I tidied up for is gone.

PARENTS

They may not be wise as the wisest, they may not
    be clever or strong.
There'll be times you will think that their counsel
    is narrow or utterly wrong.
You will think when they frown upon pleasures
    which you are so eager to share
That your father and mother who love you are
    merely an old-fashioned pair.
But this they would have you remember, whatever
    they say or they do
It is not of themselves they are thinking—their
    thoughts are all centered in you.

There are those who will flatter to please you for
    something they're eager to gain.
There are those who will seem to befriend you who
    never will constant remain.
Some stranger will lead you to folly and leave you
    the moment it's done,
Some, not caring what harm may befall you, will
    tempt you with dangerous fun,
You may question the motives of others, but remem-
    ber your whole lifetime through
Your father and mother who love you have no other
    motive than you.

There is nothing of profit they're seeking; there's
    nothing they want you to buy.
You've no reason to doubt what they tell you; they've
    nothing to gain by a lie,

Whenever they check or correct you, it is not for
    themselves that they speak,
They would happier be could they praise you, but
    it's only your welfare they seek.
You may think them old-fashioned and fussy and
    narrow, as children will do,
But remember your father and mother have all their
    hopes centered in you.

*   *   *

WONDERING

'Tis said the creatures of the field and sky
Are lost forever on the day they die.
Yet why should Heaven so sweet a joy discard
As that gay oriole singing in the yard?

If it be true, when done with earthly strife,
Mortals alone are given eternal life.
Will not the time in Heaven seem over-long
Without that little wild canary's song?

If only men at last to Heaven shall go,
There must be joys the angels want to know.
For surely with the coming of the spring
The first red robin is a Heavenly thing.

HAIL AND FAREWELL

I think of the summer cottage and the joys of the
    long years flown,
With the visits of friends, as they've come and gone
    —the friends we have loved and known.
How glad were the gay arrivals! how merry the
    smiling lips!
How blithesome the sport to meet them and carry
    in bags and grips!
But always the week-end over, how sad were the
    sigh and the smart
And the loneliness that followed as soon as they'd
    all depart!

They came with their voices ringing and smiles we
    cannot forget.
The dining room rang with their laughter, at times
    I can hear it yet.
Those days were for mirth and pleasure and free-
    dom from care and pain,
Where never a doubt should fret us and never a
    hurt remain,
But always we noticed at parting how still had the
    cottage grown
When the last good-bye had been spoken and we
    sat on the porch alone.

We looked with delight for their coming, yet al-
    ways, the truth to tell,
We knew that the hour was nearing when soon we
    must say farewell.

And that was the time we dreaded, with the still-
    ness which follows on,
When we've waved farewell at the doorway and the
    last of our friends had gone.
But the price of all joy is the sadness that comes
    when the pleasures die.
And there's never a welcome spoken but it binds us
    to say good-bye.

         ✦   ✦   ✦

GISSING'S SIXPENNY MIRACLE

George Gissing on a lovely day
    Of England's lovely spring
Chanced to encounter on his way
    A small boy sorrowing.
With head in arm against a tree
    The deeply troubled child
Wept out his heart and could not be
    Consoled or reconciled.

"I've lost the sixpence, sir," cried he,
    "Somewhere along the road
With which my parents trusted me
    To pay a bill they owed.
And it is not their rage I fear—"
    And here the youngster paused—
"But they have had too hard a year
    To stand the loss I've caused."

And Gissing as he heard him sob
    Thought in his curious way:

How strange a sixpenny piece should rob
  A boy of such a day.
Blinded by grief he cannot see
  The blossoms of the spring
Nor does he hear in every tree
  The birds that sweetly sing.

A family wretched on a day
  When earth and heaven unite
With springtime's glorious display
  Men's spirits to delight!
And then he thought "at little cost
  I'll do a wondrous thing;
I'll give him back the sixpence lost
  And give him back the spring."

✿   ✿   ✿

LUXURY

Food and raiment, health and fire
All these both rich and poor require.
What more than these the rich possess
Is luxury, not happiness.

ON LYING DOWN

If to grumbling you're inclined
　Every time a plan goes wrong,
Grumble on and ease your mind,
　But keep plodding right along.
Grit your teeth and wear a frown,
　But keep walking straight ahead.
There's no sense in lying down
　Till it's time to go to bed.

If ill luck has come your way,
　Keep on fighting as you sigh;
While with wailing loss you stay
　Life's parade goes marching by.
Never mind what's come and gone,
　Waste no time on chances fled;
Forward march and carry on.
　Do your lying down in bed!

When misfortune deals a blow,
　Be your body bruised and black,
There is just one way to go;
　There can be no turning back.
While you've strength to walk the towr
　Stand up straight and look ahead.
There's no sense in lying down
　Till it's time to go to bed.

THUMBING THROUGH LIFE

He stood upon the curbing and he waved his thumb
    at me—
A lad, perhaps of twenty, and as healthy as could be.
There was something in his manner and his most
    attractive grin
Which enticed me for the moment, so I stopped and
    took him in.

"Do many stop," I questioned, "when you're thumb-
    ing for a ride?"
"Not so many, but I stay there till one does," the
    boy replied.
"Soon or late somebody helps me, so I always wait
    about.
Will you pull up at the corner, here's the place
    where I get out."

I looked at him astounded, since so unashamed he
    talked.
He had waited to be carried seven streets he could
    have walked.
He had stood upon that corner merely jerking hand
    and thumb
Till some sympathetic driver like myself his way
    should come.

And I thought when he had left me: "Boy, with
    legs and body stout
To the goal that lies before you that's no way of
    starting out.

Here's a world that's needing action, grit and cour-
  age for the strife
And already you're believing you can thumb your
  way through life."

ஃ   ஃ   ஃ

THIS HE ASKED

This said he before he went:
  "After I am gone
Till the last of life be spent
  Let your life go on.

"Sweep the rooms and dust and bake
  As you did before.
Go you, for the children's sake,
  Smiling to the door.

"Let them dance and let them sing;
  Keep them not from play.
Grief is such a fearful thing,
  Brush its tears away.

"Wear for me your loveliest dress
  When to town you go.
You will love me none the less
  Hiding all your woe.

"Should they ask how you can be
  Serene, with heart so sore,
Say I wished in memory
  Just that—and nothing more."

PRAYER FOR STRENGTH

Not to be rid of the task,
  But the strength to perform it,
Not a weak fortress, I ask,
  But the courage to storm it!
Not the soft pillows of ease
  And the safe ways and sure,
But the outcome that no one foresees
  And the will to endure.

Not to be rid of all doubt
  But to face it unshaken.
To be able to stick the fight out
  Till the goal shall be taken.
To know the tense moments of care
  And be worn and aghast,
And then rise from the depths of despair,
  Successful at last!

Not to be rid of the strain
  And the heart-sickening minute,
But the strength and the pluck to remain
  In the fight, till I win it!
Not to be safe and secure,
  But full strength for the task
And the courage all things to endure.
  It is these that I ask.

THE PAY ENVELOPE

'Twas just a yellow envelope, not more than two by
four,
And yet it held a cottage small, with lilacs by the
door,
And meat and bread and lollypops from Burnham's
candy store.

Within that yellow envelope were frocks exceeding
fair,
A bonnet for a lovely dame and ribbons for her
hair,
And shoes of honest leather for a healthy boy to
wear.

You wouldn't think it possible that in that package
small
Were curtains for the window panes; a rug to line
the hall,
And a wedding gift for some one to be married
in the fall.

They passed it through a wicket barred and never
opened wide,
A tiny numbered envelope a toiler took with pride,
And never guessed how many splendid things were
tucked inside.

Once there was a little fellow with the laughter in
  his eye
Who was always up to nonsense when Good Sense
  was standing by.
He was always mocking Wisdom and the poses it
  would strike,
And making fun of people whom his parents seemed
  to like,
For once when he was strutting up and down like
  Banker Squeers,
His grandma caught him at it and she promptly
  boxed his ears.

He was just a little fellow who was never under-
  stood,
For he couldn't like the people that his parents
  thought he should.
And he mocked the very pious and the dignified
  and grave
Till they used to sit and wonder if he ever would
  behave.
Oft his grandma used to tell him: "If your ways
  you do not mend,
Just as sure as you are living, in a prison cell you'll
  end."

He was difficult to manage. He would ask: "Can
  Willie pitch
A wider curve than Johnny just because his father's
  rich?

Johnny's mother takes in washing, but when he
    comes up to bat
And socks it for a double no one ever thinks of
    that."
But his grandma often wondered when they'd packed
    him off to bed
How he ever got such common, vulgar notions in
    his head.

꙰   ꙰   ꙰

THE OLD HOT-DOG WAGON

Before the hot dog had grown stylish, when of
    friends it had only a few,
Before it was rigged upon toothpicks as a tidbit for
    rich folks to chew,
When I was a fledgling reporter and a nickel was
    often my all,
I used to climb into a wagon down there by the old
    City Hall,
For there about midnight for supper the boys of
    the paper would meet,
And a hot dog with mustard or radish in those days
    was something to eat.

We knew of its succulent flavor before it was known
    to the crowd.
We were the friends of the hot dog before it grew
    haughty and proud.
We sat there and talked the day over. That wagon
    with friendship was stored.

'There I first met a fellow called Henry. He told me
    his last name was Ford,
And he had the eye of a dreamer. He was making
    an automobile.
But how could we know in that wagon what time
    would so swiftly reveal?

Now the hot dog has come into fashion. It is some-
    thing on toothpicks to serve
From domes made of silver and crystal and called
    by the women hors d'oeuvre.
The wagon has gone from the corner. In wind-
    mills and castles and grills
The hot dog the countryside over entices our dimes
    into tills;
But round it no memories linger such as those which
    I fondly recall
When the boys used to meet in that wagon down
    there by the old City Hall.

FISHING

My grandfather said with a toss of his head,
    As he sat at the fire making flies,
Tying silk upon hooks for his old leather books
    And being mighty proud of his ties:
"Oh, the sport is a joy! But remember, my boy,
    Only hungry men work for the dish.
The creel's but a part of this glorious art;
    There is much more to fishing than fish.

"From spring unto fall I can answer the call
    To go out on my favorite streams,
And when wintry winds bite I can sit here at night,
    Enjoying my fancies and dreams.
For the soul can be stirred, both by blossom and bird,
    And the wonders that lie all about.
There are volumes of lore it's a joy to explore;
    Oh, there's much more to fishing than trout.

"It's not all in the catch; there's a thrill in the hatch,
    And knowing the birds by their song.
There's the tying of hooks and the reading of books,
    Which last a man all his life long;
Not a fisherman he who contented can be
    With the whirr of the reel and the swish
Of a taut running line, for the art is too fine!
    There is much more to fishing than fish."

THE ILL-TEMPERED MAN

Once in a beautiful garden where the grass was a
    carpet of green
A man in a fit of ill temper came suddenly into
    the scene.
Some trifling disturbance had happened, what it was
    I cannot now recall,
But he started to row with his neighbor and, I think,
    over nothing at all.

We were there to look over the roses, but strangely
    their beauty had fled,
As if it were frightened at hearing the words which
    were angrily said.
We had noticed a cardinal singing nearby just a
    moment before.
But the ill-tempered man started shouting and we
    heard not a golden note more.

In a garden of splendor and glory we saw but a
    man in a rage,
For beauty and loveliness vanish when men in a
    quarrel engage.
And we left there, not seeing the roses nor hearing
    the cardinal call,
For a man with a trivial grievance had ruined the
    scene for us all.

SELF-RESPECT

Now when it comes to comfort and to sleeping well
    at night,
There's nothing so important as the choice 'twixt
    wrong and right,
For there's nothing so conducive to a seven or eight
    hours' rest
As the satisfactory knowledge that you've done your
    very best.

That failure's stings are painful it is foolish to deny,
But defeat is twice as bitter when you know you
    didn't try,
And the victory that's ill-gotten brings no gain that's
    worth the cost
When you lie awake remembering that your self-
    respect you've lost.

In the moments of temptation be not hasty to decide.
Is a temporary conquest worth a lifetime's loss of
    pride?
If you do the best you can do, though your pocket-
    book is light,
You can walk the world undaunted and can go to
    sleep at night.

UPSY-DAISY

Oft my father used to say:
  "Never mind that little fall!
Soon the pain will pass away.
  Pretend it doesn't hurt at all.
Men like you and me must bear
  Many a blow from day to day.
Upsy-Daisy! Don't you care!
  You just run along and play."

Swiftly time went winging by.
  Thus I spoke to him, when he
Puckered up his lips to cry,
  Carrying his hurts to me:
"Come! let's get those teardrops dried.
  Run along, my boy, and play!
Men like you and me must hide
  Many a pain that comes our way.

"Upsy-Daisy! Now and go
  Back to play without a word!
Join your friends again as though
  Such a bump had not occurred.
Men like you and me must keep
  Unobserved the pain we bear,
Covering our bruises deep,
  Just as though we didn't care."

So my father talked to me,
  So I tried my boy to train;

So instructed lads will be
  Till no more on earth remain.
"Upsy-Daisy! Off you go
  Back again to work or play.
Men like you and me must know
  Many a bruise along the way!"

    ❧   ❧   ❧

ALL IN THE DAY'S WORK

"All in the day's work!" someone said.
  "All in the day's work!" one replied.
And as to smile he turned his head
  Somewhere that minute people died.

Somewhere that moment babes were born.
  Somewhere were many suffering pain.
For some it was a wedding morn,
  For others one of loss or gain.

Somewhere moved chance or accident
  To prosper men or dash them low.
Somewhere transpired the least event
  And greatest mortals live to know.

Somewhere were laughter, mirth and song.
  Somewhere as swiftly moments fled
Mankind encountered right and wrong,
  "All in the day's work," as he said.

FLIRTATION

As I was walking down the street
  As pious as could be,
A pretty girl I chanced to meet
  Who winked her eye at me.

My foolish age has long flown by
  And I am fat and staid,
And it's been many years since I
  Have flirted with a maid.

My mind was on the day's affairs,
  Which I should soon discuss,
As with my very gravest airs
  I strode toward a bus.

But fifty-four I find is not
  Immune to woman's wiles,
Although 'tis true I had forgot
  How dangerous are her smiles.

And suddenly I chanced to see
  This siren on my track,
So when the maiden winked at me
  I winked the lady back.

Although I was on business bent,
  To chat with her I stayed,
Which shows how men of good intent
  By woman can be swayed.

She stuck me for an ice cream cone
  Then ran along to play,
And left me there to wait alone
  For the bus to come my way.

MEN SHE COULD HAVE MARRIED

I have heard great tales of their kindly ways,
　And the things they did and the things they
　　wouldn't;
The years have lacquered them deep with praise.
　They have gained the unchangeable worth I
　　couldn't.
Could I trace them down they must all be great.
　Unless, like mine, have their plans miscarried.
But still, whatever has been their fate,
　They live as the fellows she could have married.

They were thoughtful men, all the handsome lot.
　They danced and they sang and their jokes were
　　clever.
Birthdays and feast days they never forgot.
　Their like upon earth will be known here never.
Though little of splendor I used to see
　In the days when about her door they tarried,
They have lived to be spoken of now to me
　"As the marvelous men that she could have mar-
　　ried."

Not one of them ugly or poor or stout!
　Not one of them foolish or dull or hairless!
Not one with a blemish worth pointing out!
　Not one of them even the least bit careless!
And I wonder at times how it came to be
　The ardor of gents like that she parried,
And went to the altar at last with me
　Instead of those marvels she could have married.

THE MOTHER

She never left the children all alone to get their tea.
At home to put the kettle on she always wished to
be.
The time we took a holiday and went to see the
Fair,
She talked about the children and kept wishing they
were there.

There wasn't any pleasure worth the worrying, she
said.
She never seemed contented till she'd tucked them
all in bed.
As they were growing older she made this her rigid
rule,
To be on hand to greet them when they all came
home from school.

She never wanted pleasures that her family couldn't
share.
She only wanted pretty things for those she loved to
wear,
For her heart was with her children, and when came
the time to roam
If she couldn't take them with her, she would rather
stay at home.

She liked to get their suppers just to know how they
were fed.
She had the notion others wouldn't care what prayers
they said.

And still serenely happy and as proud as proud
    can be,
She likes to put the kettle on when they come home
    for tea.

        ❧   ❧   ❧

TWO SOURCES OF WEALTH

Wealth comes out of the earth, they say—
    The golden grain and the metals cold.
Out of the ground comes the toiler's pay.
    Out of the ground comes the rich man's gold.

Then whence come laughter and lilting song,
    And whence come friendships for men to find?
Whence comes choice between right and wrong?
    Out of the heart and out of the mind.

Two real sources of wealth has man;
    But over the earth may the tempest sweep
And the riches gathered by pick and pan
    Are easier found than they are to keep.

But that other wealth of the heart and mind
    Which is coined in wisdom and mirth and song
And makes man friendly and makes him kind
    Enriches him for his whole life long.

WOMEN

More and more the women try me
With their "what ye goin' to buy me?"
And their everlasting wanting
  This and that;
With their all-consuming passion
To be what they call "in fashion,"
From the buckles on their slippers
  To the hat.

Seems that every week they trim me
With their "gimme," "gimme," "gimme,"
And the artful way they work it
  Makes me smile!
Though I like 'em looking pretty,
Still I wish they'd have some pity;
But there's nothing so hard-hearted
  As the style.

There are times I think I oughter
Tell that doting wife and daughter
When they gently run their fingers
  Through my hair,
And they bend a bit above me
Just to say how much they love me,
That I will not buy another
  Dress to wear.

But I don't; the plain fact this is,
Though I know their hugs and kisses

Will be followed by the "gimme"
  I condemn,
Still I let them put it over
And I hope they won't discover
That my greatest joy is buying
  Things for them.

❧ ❧ ❧

WEEDS

What cruel savages are weeds!
  Let but the friend of flowers depart
  They'll stab the roses to the heart
And slash at beauty till it bleeds.

They'll rush the parapet and gate
  To get where lovely things are grown
  And with a fury all their own
Will leave the garden desolate.

They'll smother with demoniac glee
  The zinnia and the marigold;
  With cunning and with daring bold
They'll throttle all that's fair to see.

Turning your back for but a week
  Upon the garden that you keep
  The savage weeds on it will leap
And leave its lovely pathways bleak.

TO THE FATHER

He has comrades eight or ten for the games you
    cannot share;
If he needs a second baseman he can find one any-
    where.
You have grown too old to play and you're much
    too fat to run.
You have come to middle age and his youth has
    just begun,
So don't try to be his pal. You will better serve the
    lad
If you'll be content to be just his understanding Dad.

He'll have friends where'er he goes, just as you did
    years ago,
And perhaps they'll talk of things they may not
    want you to know.
There are others of his age who will keep him com-
    pany,
But there's something he'll require only you have
    power to be.
You've a higher place to fill. Pals can everywhere
    be had.
What that youngster wants and needs is an under-
    standing Dad.

Be his father! That's enough! When his time of
    play is through,
Let him know whate'er betide he may safely come
    to you.

Be the father unto whom he can tell his every need
And be sure of sympathy, for it's that he's bound to
   need.
You are old and he is young. Mark the difference
   and be glad.
He may never want for pals, but he'll often want
   his Dad.

❧   ❧   ❧

FIRST LOOK AT THE BABY

Over the bassinet
   Now we stand peeping,
Trying our best
   Just to gaze at him sleeping.

Into our arms they say
   No one may take him.
Far must we stand away
   Lest we should wake him.

Inch back the covers now,
   Soft fold and wimple!
Gaze at his father's brow!
   Chin with a dimple!

Face of his mother fair!
   Like her he may be.
Oh, what a wealth of hair!
   Oh, what baby!

169

ORPHANS OF THE LIVING

We think of orphans only as the little girls and lads
Who haven't any mothers or who haven't any dads.
They are grouped with other children and in groups
    they're put to bed
With some stranger, paid to listen, when their little
    prayers are said.
All the grownups look with pity on such lonely
    children small
And declare to be an orphan is the saddest fate
    of all.

But sometimes I look about me and in sorrow hang
    my head
As I gaze on something sadder than the orphans of
    the dead.
For more pitiful and tragic, as the long days come
    and go,
Are the orphans of the parents they are not allowed
    to know.
They're the orphans of the living, left alone to
    romp and play,
From their fathers and their mothers by ambition
    shut away.

They have fathers who are busy and so weighted
    down with cares
That they haven't time to listen to a little child's
    affairs.
They have mothers who imagine life could give
    them if it would

Something richer, something better than the joys of
  motherhood.
So their children learn from strangers and by
  strangers' hands are fed,
And the nurse, for so much money, nightly tucks
  them into bed.

Lord, I would not grow so busy that I cannot drop
  my task
To answer every question which that child of mine
  can ask.
Let me never serve ambition here so selfishly, I
  pray,
That I cannot stop to listen to the things my children
  say.
For whatever cares beset them, let them know I'm
  standing by.
I don't want to make them orphans till the day I
  come to die.

THE ORDINARY MAN'S ADVENTURE

Not all adventure lies afar. 'Tis something day by
day
At adding figures in a book devotedly to stay.
Though dreams are built on luxury, the facts of life
are stern,
And many a man must shape his ends to what his
strength can earn.
Not all the heroes warriors are. Courageous hearts
and stout
Go bravely to adventures that are seldom talked
about.

He had this problem day by day, to clothe his chil-
dren small;
To keep a roof above their heads and educate them
all.
The mother shared adventure, too. So much do
youngsters ask
To keep them glad to be at home was not an easy
task.
Yet here's the glory of their lives! I cite it as a fact.
Through difficulty and despair that home was kept
intact.

Against the odds they bravely fought and as the chil-
dren grew
Always, in spite of poverty, some happiness they
knew.
Planning and toiling for their needs they labored
side by side,

And lived to look across the years at last with joy
    and pride.
This their achievement: children grown to men and
    women good.
This their adventure: they had done with life the
    best they could.

          ❧   ❧   ❧

STRENGTH

He who has strength for the task
Has all that a man need ask.
He who can rise with the day,
Ready and fit for the fray,
Has that to encounter his foe
Which is better than luck can bestow.

He who can go to his trade
Clear-eyed, alert, unafraid,
Knowing that he can outstay
The grind and the heat of day,
Has more in his power to advance
Than those who are trusting to chance.

He who has knowledge and skill
And the strength for his task and the will;
And from dawn to the day's weary end
On himself with good faith can depend
Has more, as the weeks come and go,
Than luck has the power to bestow.

PREPARATIONS FOR DEPARTURE

Mother's busy buying ribbons now for little Janet's
    hair,
And several sorts of dresses for the two of them to
    wear.
She goes shopping every morning at a most terrific
    speed,
Stocking up with countless stockings, which she says
    they'll surely need.
They are dated at the parlors where the beauty stuff
    is sold,
And these days of preparation are not long enough,
    I'm told.

The trunk is in the hallway, but as far as I can see
Not a single hanger in it has been set aside for me.
It's already stuffed with dresses and I'm trying to
    compute
Sufficient space within it that will hold my Sunday
    suit.
If I say: "This trunk seems crowded," mother gives
    her head a shake
And informs me: "That is only stuff we've simply
    got to take!"

There are boxes on the tables filled with things
    they're going to use.
There are plain and fancy slippers and a fine array
    of shoes.
There are various kinds of "pretties" (proper names
    to me unknown),

But the fluffy, ruffled garments every woman loves
to own,
And I sometimes stand and wonder as this mass of
stuff I see
Where she'll pack the socks and neckties that must
go along for me.

These are days of keen excitement, as may easily be
guessed.
When they get to California they're both to look
their best.
They are trying on their dresses and then stowing
them away,
Just as busy as the farmers when it's time for mak-
ing hay.
But last night I said to mother just as gently as I
could:
"Was it you or I or Janet got this call to Holly-
wood?"

AN OLD EMPLOYER TALKS

To a long-time employer I went and inquired:
"What can you tell me of boys you have hired?
Down through the years you've had many pass by,
And a few have succeeded, but do you know why?
Have you some jobs here so hidden from view
That a youngster is lost 'spite of all he may do?"

"Well!" he replied. "From the wheelbarrow line
Less than three years ago came that foreman of mine.
Look through that panel. Out there is a clerk
Already preparing to flee from his work.
Now watch him at quitting time rush for his hat.
Would you for promotion pick someone like that?

"He thinks he's not noticed. Well, now, let me
      show
Just how thoroughly well that young fellow I know.
At ten minutes to five, with his eye on the clock,
The drawer at the right of his desk he'll unlock
And that task, still unfinished, he'll stow away flat,
To be ready to spring, at the bell, for his hat.

"Now, that fellow's faithful, correct as a clerk,
But deep in his heart there's no love for the work.
He fancies, no doubt, that he hasn't a chance,
That from tasks such as his one can never advance.
Yet the fact he forgets as he frets in his chair
Is that many a big man today started there."

OF SUCH STUFF IS MEMORY

Memories are made of these:
  Little words the babies say;
  Games, which now and then we play;
  Grandpas and their manners quaint;
  China, grandmas used to paint;
  Grace which mother always said,
  Thankful for our daily bread.
  These the memory will hold
  To be joyously retold.

Memories are made of these:
  Days when skies were overcast;
  Strange adventures of the past;
  Difficulties met somehow,
  Tragic then, but comic now;
  All the curious mistakes
  Everybody living makes.
  These the big things after all
  That we tenderly recall.

Memories are made of these:
  Small mishaps from year to year;
  Little whims of someone dear;
  Tunes that someone used to play,
  Now forever gone away;
  Favorite jokes the father told,
  Young today, but then so old!
  These, when time has cast its spell,
  We shall joyously retell.

THE YOUNGEST CHILD

I'm told by good authority
That it is difficult to be
The youngest child and stand about
To see the elder ones go out
To dinners, dances and to shows
And be the one who never goes.

'Tis rather hard, as I've been told,
To be eleven or twelve years old
And still be much too young to do
So many things you're wanting to;
To see the others gayly roam
And always have to stay at home.

I know by evidence compiled
'Tis hard to be the youngest child,
This sentence doomed always to know:
"Of course, my dear, you cannot go!
Your brother's going? That may be,
But you are not as old as he."

By doleful wails and plaints and sighs
I'm told injustice underlies
The joys of childhood. Being small
Is not a bit of fun at all!
Take it from protests daily filed,
It's hard to be the youngest child.

NOT SO FAST!

"Not so fast!" said I, but he,
Just a little chap of three,
Laughed away my word of warning
Till he fell and bruised his knee.
"Not so fast!" said I once more
When the little tyke was four,
"Just be careful when you're running
It's a very slippery floor."

"Not so fast!" I told him when
He was eight and nine and ten,
But old age with all its caution
Couldn't slow those flying feet,
And in vain with him I'd plead
For he never seemed to heed,
Since the urge to run was in him
And the joy of it was sweet.

Shall we never learn to heed?
Are we children all who need
Someone constantly to warn us
Of this dangerous love of speed?
All in vain must someone cry,
"Not so fast!" as we go by?
Must we laugh at all the warnings
Till the day we come to die?

LOSS

Loss is a word of ache and smart.
   Its every use implies
A stinging bitterness of heart.
   Even the scholars wise
Who tear our common speech apart
   Find in it only sighs.

The lexicographers declare,
   Out of their wisdom deep,
That loss is linked to treasures rare
   Which we have failed to keep,
Producing anguish hard to bear
   And causing us to weep.

And so it is. Yet as I muse
   Today in moments sad,
I find whene'er that word I use
   It is not wholly bad;
Because the treasure that I lose,
   Long time or brief I've had.

And so if firm be our belief
   When comes the cruel test,
The more we suffer in our grief,
   The more have we been blessed.
Loss writes on life's long ledger leaf
   The riches once possessed.

FLATTERERS

If it's flattery you want, you must always stay on
    top;
Never lose a little battle, never let your credit drop.
For the flatterers only swarm where triumphant men
    are found.
When it's faith and help you need they will never
    be around.

If it's flattery you seek, keep your pockets filled with
    gold.
Single-handed you must fight if the flatterers you'd
    hold.
Single-handed you must bear every burden on you
    laid,
For the flatterers will desert if you ever call for aid.

If it's flattery you want, make yourself so very wise
That you'll find the grain of truth underneath a
    thousand lies.
Never falter. Never fail. Never wince where men
    can see.
For where doubt and danger threat flatterers do not
    care to be.

If you must always be praised, whether false or
    whether true,
Be assured that you can brave every care that comes
    to you.
Be assured that you are safe from whate'er the fates
    may send,

For the flatterers will have fled should you ever need
a friend.

❧ ❧ ❧

THE LITTLE STREETS

Accidents will happen, •but still many of them
shouldn't.
With just a little thought and care 'tis certain that
they wouldn't.
The streets are made for traffic, but what motorist
can say
He doesn't know the little streets are where the
children play?

'Tis hard to teach a tiny tot who has no ground to
play on
That when his ball rolls in the street the curbing he
must stay on;
And yet it harder seems to be to teach some drivers
wild
That they must watch the little streets or they may
kill a child.

Sometimes the youngsters are to blame. They're
thoughtless and they're dareful,
But it's a grown-up's duty while he's driving to be
careful.
And every driver of a car unto himself should say:

"The little residential streets are where the children
  play!"

I've little patience with the man who down some
  road goes humming
And leaves it to the children to know just how fast
  he's coming.
I think the task of watchfulness the grown-ups ought
  to bear,
And when they drive the little streets, look out for
  children there.

＊　＊　＊

LIFE

Life looked at me and said:
When do the countless dead
Speak or enjoy an hour,
Know bird or bee or flower,
Laughter or merry song,
Streams as they flash along,
Woods and their cooling shade,
Winter's severe brigade,
Summer or spring or fall
Or voices of friends who call?

Over each silent mound
Myrtle and grass are wound;
Near by with every spring
Birds come to mate and sing;
Tulip and hyacinth grace
Man's final resting place,
But these charms richly spread

Cannot delight the dead.
Joys for the living these
Glories and harmonies.

Know them the while you may
Ere you shall pass away.
Speak now the kindly word
While it can still be heard.
Love bird and flower and tree
While you may hear and see.
Live to your blithest, best.
Leaving to God the rest.
Death is another birth
Far from the realms of earth.

INDEX TO FIRST LINES

Index of First Lines

Index of First Lines

Index of First Lines

Index of First Lines

Index of First Lines

Index of First Lines

Index of First Lines